project
for
BUILDERS and CONTRACTORS

Norman Willoughby

Published by NWM Ltd.
1995

© Copyright Norman Willoughby 1995

All rights reserved

No part of this book may be reproduced or transmitted in any form by any means including graphic, electronic or mechanical or by any information storage or retrieval system, without prior permission of the publisher except for brief passages quoted in a review.

Canadian Cataloguing in Publication Data

Willoughby, Norman 1927 -
Project Management for Builders and Contractors

Includes Index
ISBN 0-9698126-1-2

1. Construction industry --Management. 2. Industrial project management. I. Title.
TH438.W54 1995   624'.068   C95-911094-1

Published by:
NWM Ltd
Box 48126
3575 Douglas Street
Victoria, B.C.,
Canada, V8Z 7H5

Enquiries to the above address.

This is a book about project management designed to provide information on that subject based on the training and experience of the author. Neither the author nor the publisher pretends to offer legal advice or advice on other professional specializations. If such advice is required, it is recommended that the reader seek it from the properly qualified professional authority.

By the same author: *incredibly easy project management* ISBN 0-9698126-0-4

Printed in Canada

In memory of my father
who is responsible for all my **good** ideas

Acknowledgements:
To all those who bought
incredibly easy project management
and rationalised why
to their cost
they could ignore its advice
or who disregarded its axioms
may this one keep it company
on your bookshelf

Thank you to John Staley for advice on book design
and to Mary for serenely suffering my insouciance

They who set themselves to give precepts must of course regard themselves as possessed of greater skill than those to whom they prescribe; and if they err in the slightest particular they subject themselves to censure. But as this tract is put forth merely as a history, or, if you will, as a tale, in which, amid some examples worthy of imitation, there will. be found, perhaps, as many more which it were not advisable to follow, I hope it will prove useful to some without being hurtful to any, and that my openness will find some favour with all.

René Descartes - Discourse on the Method of Rightly Conducting the Reason, and Finding Truth in the Sciences

project management for
Builders and Contractors

The book is in 4 sections; an Outline that covers all the **essentials;** the same subjects in more **detail,** followed by even **greater detail** and a Section containing examples of the **documents** recommended and an **appendix** containing what you may conclude are some of the more obscure elements of project management.

INTRODUCTION
What is a Project Manager?

SECTION 1 - AN OUTLINE
The Essentials
Planning
Execution
Evaluation
Definitions

SECTION 2 - SOME DETAIL
Planning
Project Execution
Evaluation

SECTION 3 - MORE DETAIL
Project Planning
Contract Documents
Estimating
Work Breakdown Structure
Coordination & Interfaces
Supervision
Contracts
Construction Management
Quality Assurance
Project Execution and Completion
Follow-Up
Dealing with Consultants
Control
Evaluation

SECTION 4 - DOCUMENTS
Contracts and Other Formats

APPENDICES

INDEX

Detailed "Contents" on the following pages.

CONTENTS

INTRODUCTION
What is a Project Manager?   12

SECTION 1 - AN OUTLINE

THE ESSENTIALS	14
ATTITUDE	14
PRECISION	15
COMMUNICATION	15
PLANNING	**16**
PROJECT MANAGEMENT TERMS	16
PLAN OF OPERATION	18
EXECUTION	**19**
EVALUATION	**19**
SUMMARY	**20**
FIRST STEPS	20
DURING EXECUTION	21
AFTER COMPLETION	21
DEFINITIONS FOR BUILDERS	**21**
PROJECT MGMNT. DEFINITIONS	**23**
BUSINESS PROMOTION	**26**

SECTION 2 - SOME DETAIL

PLANNING	**28**
STRATEGIC PLAN	28
Goal	29
Purpose	30
STRATEGIC PLAN OUTLINE	31
PLAN OF OPERATION	31
CONTROL	34
PROJECT EXECUTION	**35**
COORDINATION	35
SUPERVISION	35
PROJECT COMPLETION	36
FOLLOW UP	37
EVALUATION	**37**
PROJECT EVALUATION	37
STRATEGIC EVALUATION	38

SECTION 3 - MORE DETAIL

PROJECT PLANNING	**39**
PLAN OF OPERATION	39
BUDGET	41
LOGICAL FRAMEWORK ANALYSIS	42
ORGANIGRAM (Organization Chart)	44
SCHEDULE	48
Network Diagrams	51
CONTRACT DOCUMENTS	**51**
PLANS AND SPECIFICATIONS	52
SCOPE OF WORK - Work Description	54
More on the Scope of Work	55
Related Work	59
Exclusions	60
Scope of Work for Large Contracts	60
Acceptable Legal Contract Format	61
COST OF THE WORK	62
SHOP DRAWINGS	63
"AS-BUILT" DOCUMENTS	64
SAMPLES	64
CONTRACT DOC. INTERPRETATION	65
ESTIMATING	**66**
METHODS	66
OVERHEAD	67
CONTINGENCIES	69
Builder Contingency	69
Client Contingency	71
BUDGET - ACCOUNTS	**72**
WORK BREAKDOWN STRUCTURE	**73**
WORK BREAKDOWN (WBS) BASICS	75
OTHER INFORMATION IN THE WBS	80
SUMMARY OF THE WBS	82
Administration	84
Contracting	85
Site Control	85
Budget and Resources	86
APPROVALS	**87**
COORDINATION & INTERFACES	**88**
SITE COORDINATION MEETING	88
INTERFACES for Additions & Renovations	88
LABOUR-ONLY CONTRACTS	89
INSPECTIONS AND APPROVALS	89
CONTRACT ADMIN DOCUMENTS	89
SUPERVISION	**89**
PLANNING	89
PROJECT DIARY	91

CONTRACTS	**91**
CLIENT	92
SUB-CONTRACTORS	93
SUPPLIERS	94
EMPLOYEES	94
SUMMARY	94
CONTRACT TYPES	**95**
STIPULATED PRICE	95
COST PLUS	96
TIME AND MATERIAL	97
TIME AND MATERIAL PLUS FEE	97
CHANGES AND INSTRUCTIONS	**97**
SITE INSTRUCTION	98
CHANGE ORDER	98
CHANGE ORDERS IN CM	98
REQUEST FOR CHANGE	99
CONSTRUCTION MANAGEMENT	**99**
QUALITY CONTROL	101
GENERAL CONTRACTOR AS CM	101
FEE STRUCTURE	102
CONFLICT WITHIN CM	103
CM AND THE SMALL BUILDER	105
QUALITY ASSURANCE	**105**
DEFINITION	106
QUALITY ASSURANCE for the CM	108
QUALITY ASSURANCE for the Builder/Contractor	109
QUALITY ASSURANCE for the CM and General Contractor	109
QUALITY ASSURANCE for Client & CM	109
COST OF QUALITY ASSURANCE	110
PERSONNEL QUALIFICATIONS	110
FACTORY INSPECTIONS	111
EXECUTION	**112**
COORDINATION	112
INTERFACES in Program Environments	113
SUPERVISION	114
INSPECTION	115
PROJECT COMPLETION	**118**
COMMISSIONING	118
DEFICIENCIES & INCOMPLETE WORK	120
VALUATION OF DEFICIENCIES	121
Deficiencies and Sub-contractors	121
Deficiencies in CM	122
Back-charges	122

FOLLOW-UP   123
FOLLOW-UP, CATEGORY 1   123
FOLLOW-UP, CATEGORY 2   124
FOLLOW-UP, CATEGORY 3   124
FOLLOW-UP, CATEGORY 4   125
DEALING WITH CONSULTANTS   **125**
CONTROL   **126**
CONTROL CRITERIA   126
EVALUATION   **127**
BUDGET   127
ORGANIGRAM   127
WORK BREAKDOWN STRUCTURE   128
SCHEDULE   128
CONTRACTS   128
CONTRACT WARRANTIES   128
LOGICAL FRAMEWORK ANALYSIS   128

SECTION 4 - DOCUMENTS

CONTRACTS   **129**
STIPULATED PRICE   130
STIPULATED PRICE PLUS FEE   153
PROPOSAL AS A CONTRACT   157

CHANGE ORDER   **160**
CHANGE ORDER FORMAT   162
ADMIN. COST OF A CHANGE ORDER   163

SITE INSTRUCTION   **164**

PURCHASE ORDER   **166**

PLAN OF OPERATION   **167**

APPENDIX 1-Logical Framework Analysis   169
APPENDIX 2- Work Breakdown Structure   172

INDEX

INTRODUCTION

This manual is written to serve equally the builder of small projects (additions, renovations, one or two houses, etc.) as well as respectfully offering some advice that it is hoped will be found useful to multi-project and mega-project contractors.

The principles of project management are the same no matter how much business you may do. If you can make a hash of a small project you can probably do the same to a large one - with much more disastrous results. And every small builder hopes to become big enough to have that opportunity.

A large builder that does not plan well may be able to survive a failed project. But can the small builder afford to lose a month's salary because his/her agreement is weak or faulty or non-existent? It is more likely to happen if you don't have a **written** contract - as complete a contract as you can make it. The contract format offered in Section 4 is equally useful to **all** builders. All builders, large and small should consider very carefully the requirement for a contract for **every** project.

I repeat, the **principles** of management are identical for all builders. You cannot afford to ignore them and you cannot afford not to apply them. Loss of a thousand dollars can be as devastating to a small operator as a hundred thousand dollars to a larger. Good project management increases your chance of success.

You may already find that I am telling you things that you have suspected or known for a long time. If that is true, then you should be doing them.

If you have felt uncomfortable at leaving your sub-contractors to work alone and unsupervised, if you have had to foot the bill after the project was complete, for something that was omitted; if the Client tells you that he didn't want it done *that* way; if you get the feeling that no-one is listening, then you have the same problems as all builders and it is time you started to *think in project management terms*.

That shouldn't worry you. Project Management is simply the application of common-sense and orderliness to everyday short and long-term problems. There is a slightly more complex definition later in the book but this is the truth of the matter. Apply the **principles** outlined in this book and you will soon have your projects under control. Being in full **control** means benefitting from your own success - it also means taking **responsibility** for your own failure!

What is a Project Manager?

If you are a builder, you may be wondering how useful project management can be to you and if its techniques are necessary. You may be a small company or an individual, interested only in house renovations or additions and conclude that only multi-project builders or contractors need to bother with project management. But continue reading and decide for yourself.

You think of yourself as a builder or contractor, but .... do you find yourself doing the things that a *Project Manager* does?

The Project Manager	**The Builder**
• finds the client	♦ you advertise or get a referral
• submits a proposal	♦ tell them what it is and what it will cost
• commissions design	♦ get someone to do a drawing
• obtains approvals of authorities having jurisdiction	♦ get a permit and call for an inspection
• develops a contract and a description of the work	♦ maybe you don't do this - but you should
• sometimes arranges financing	♦ visit your friendly bank
• plans (systematizes) the project	♦ call your subs and hope they arrive when they say they will
• coordinates execution of the project	♦ make sure they don't put the drywall on before the electrician has finished
• develops interfaces between trades	♦ avoid having two Subs working in the same space at the same time
• monitors the execution of the work	♦ spend more time at the site than you would like
• liaises with the client	♦ talk to the Client when you **must**
• manages procurement	♦ visit your suppliers
• evaluates his/her work and	♦ well, that didn't go so well, did it?
• makes changes to his/her **strategic plan** based on project performance.	♦ decide not to do it that way again.

If you do the things in the left column, then you **know** you are a Project Manager. And if you do the things in the right column, you **are** a Project Manager - like it or not - and you **should** be managing your projects in a professional manner. In fact, the builder, including the home construction, renovation or addition contractor may justifiably claim to be the authentic, **complete** project manager.

Simply **doing** these things is not enough. To benefit to the maximum from your activities, they must be done within a proper framework and in a proper manner. A framework, a proper format or **plan** (Plan of Operation) will give consistency of execution to each project and enable you to analyze your problems and improve your performance and that of your employees and sub-contractors on subsequent projects.

Projects come in all sizes but no project is too small to be attempted without a framework or plan - or of too small a value not to require a *written* plan

Your **"attitude"** toward your project, your Client, your sub-contractors and others through the three principal stages, Planning, Execution and Evaluation will determine whether or not the project is a success.

> A small Builder for whom I had performed some services was telling me of a $7,000 project that he was about to start. I asked if he had a written contract. "No", he replied, "but it is only a small job and the Owner is in a hurry". I shook my head resignedly but did not press the issue. Four months later Tom was in small-claims court, trying to collect the balance of $2,000. He got it after a lot of hard work and lost time through attendance at court. But he learned his lesson. Now he is a preferred client - for a very small investment he writes a form of contract for everything he builds, no matter the price of the work; he has had no legal problems since.

CONSTRUCTION NOTE

In Southern Portugal's Algarve, most residential construction is of masonry infill to structural concrete framing, all plastered inside and out. It is commonplace for roof or balcony drainage to be installed **after** basic construction is complete. This is done with the nonchalant use of a jack-hammer; blasting through walls, beams, stair structure and anything else that gets in the way. Because Portuguese masons do a good job of plastering, everything is neatly covered. Advice - do not watch your house being built in the Algarve.

BUSINESS NOTE

A well-established contractor was persuaded to sell his business. The buyers knew that he had valuable public works contracts about to start, that several lucrative contracts were under way and the company's reputation would bring in more. All the negotiations were complete except for the settlement of outstanding accounts (a considerable sum). Late in the day that the transfer of ownership was to be signed the current owner presented himself at the lawyers' office displaying cheque stubs showing all sums due had been paid. The new owners accepted this and made their final payment. Good wishes all round and the original owner left for the airport. That was Friday. On Monday it was discovered that none of the cheques matching the stubs had been issued!

SECTION 1

AN OUTLINE

THE ESSENTIALS

- **Attitude** - think and act professionally
- **Precision** - no detail is too small
- **Communication** - is the responsibility of the Project Manager

ATTITUDE

In **all** project management, including project management of construction, in all **stages** of project management, the most important consideration in the management of a project is **"attitude"** - the "attitude" of the Project Manager and the Management Team (if there is a Team). The project must be approached in a professional manner. If you want a successful, profitable project, then a small project requires as much care as does a large one. The **quantity** of information required may be less but all the **elements** of a good project plan must be there. Don't neglect to pay attention to the essential steps because the project costs less or has a lower profile than others on your agenda. You will not spend as much time on a small project but you must maintain the same meticulous approach.

It is essential to approach the requirements of project management in general and those of each project in particular with the certain conviction that **you** can make it succeed or fail and to accept full responsibility for its success or failure.

Only *you* can make the project succeed or allow it to fail

When I suggest that the key to successful project management is **attitude,** I mean more than simply **looking** like a good manager (a lot of talk and activity) I am referring to a real dedication to the spirit of good management - the ambition to get it right, to suffer the personal inconveniences necessary to get the job done and the willingness to risk your popularity. It is a question of really **believing** in what you are doing.

PRECISION

You must be meticulous in all aspects of your work. It is easy enough if you are that type of person (a nit-picker, perhaps?) but most of us have to force ourselves to pay attention to detail. It is particularly difficult for builders, who seem to spend most of their time up to the hips in alligators with little opportunity to check and double-check, to make sure that everyone on the project is carrying out his or her task, to do the essential paper work and to keep the Client up-to-date.

Nevertheless, lack of precision will get you into trouble. Think not only in general terms but in terms of detail. It is the small problems ignored that will trigger a chain of increasingly large problems that will ruin the project and cost you money. I repeat, it is the little things that will kill the project. The old adage *"for the want of a nail the horse was lost, for the want of a horse the battle was lost"* is true of projects - and of nails!

> **Projects rarely fail because of a major calamity**
> **but are nibbled to death by small omissions**

COMMUNICATION

If I had not already said that "attitude" is the most important element of project management, I would say it about "communication". Unless the information that you have, as Project Manager (PM), is distributed at the right time to the right person, nothing will happen as it should. Equally important is that you receive information that you need at the right time and in a suitable format.

It is the obligation of the PM to make sure that **effective** communication happens as it should, both sending it out and receiving it. You cannot excuse yourself by saying "So-and-so did not tell me in time!". **You** must know what information is required, when it is required and must badger someone to death to make sure that you get it. No excuses! This is part of the "attitude". Do not try to be popular. You are trying to do a good job. Be as pleasant as you can be but make sure the information flows.

> ***You*, and only you, are responsible for**
> **communication flow**

> At regular weekly meetings on a multi-million dollar Government project, it became increasingly obvious that information was not getting to the right people. Without telling the PM, I instructed the secretarial staff to deliver all the mail to me. Every day I reviewed it, marked it for response by "X", copies to "Y" and "Z", etc. and indicated dates for compliance. Although I had exceeded my authority (I was Contracts Manager), there was some muttering but no substantial complaints. Effective communication had been established.

The various stages of project management are dependent first on **attitude**, on **precision** and on **communication**. If you accept that, and before we get into the practicalities and details of managing construction projects, we shall first take a broad view of the fundamentals of:

- **Planning**
- **Execution**
- **Evaluation**

PLANNING

SUMMARY of PLANNING TERMS	
Goal	Your long-term target
Purpose	Why you are building the project?
Outputs	The **product** resulting from Planning & Execution.
Inputs	What the Plan tells you to put into the product.

The next couple of pages may not be fascinating but please read them just to become familiar with the terms. There is nothing here that you do not already know either by instinct or experience.

PROJECT MANAGEMENT TERMS

Planning is the stage at which a project may be most easily ruined. Good planning is the foundation-stone of good execution. But planning and execution should never be divorced from each other. Keep in mind as you plan the project, that **you** have to follow the plan (Plan of Operation) and make it work. Never make it more complicated than you can handle and still do a good job; your capacity for carrying out the plan must be equal to what you have planned.

**Your ability to carry out the plan
must not be less than what you have planned**

The key to successful planning is more a combination lock than one key. But an important element of the combination, whether the project is large or small, is logical thought. Because the thoughts must be successfully communicated (remember that "communication" is important), it is easier to stick to accepted methods and terms. Bear with me while we look **briefly** at these terms. You need to know them but not be overwhelmed by them.

    Goal is generally accepted as a broad, "strategic" objective into which a project fits - the end result of the years you are going to work as a builder.

    Purpose is the end objective of the *project* that, in the long-term, contributes to the Goal.

    Output(s) is the product resulting from the execution of the project - a building, an extension, a highway, a tourist development, etc.

    Input(s) is the requirement of service, finance and material that will produce the Output or project. You will see in *Section 2 (Strategic Plan)* how "Input" leads to "Output", up to "Purpose" and so to "Goal".

    The diagram below shows that, for the Builder, the immediately important terms are **Output** and **Input** if you consider that Inputs are what you put into a project (logical?) and Outputs are what you get out (more logic). Broadly speaking your Inputs are material, labour and management. Your Outputs are a building, an addition, a renovation or some other physical thing plus a profit. You could also consider "goodwill" as an output; it has a monetary value and sometimes (perhaps, too often) takes the place of profit. Purpose and Goal will be dealt with later.

STRATEGIC PLAN	Goal	
	Purpose	Purpose eventually & cumulatively achieves Goal
PROJECT PLAN	Output	Outputs lead to the Purpose
	Input	Inputs provide the output above

PLAN OF OPERATION

The Plan of Operation (POP) tells you how you are going to carry out the project and should tell you what you are going to get out of it. It can be a complex document or a simple one or it may just exist in your head. But, if you want a successful project, a profitable project .... **put it on paper**.

A *written* Plan is the best Plan

This is a bold step for a lot of small builders but it won't hurt to try it. You can make it simple to start with and, when you discover that it helps (as it surely will), you can make it more detailed for the next project.

The Plan of Operation should also contain or refer to the documentation that describes the project. The most important of these is a contract with the Client but there should also be contracts with Sub-contractors, appropriate drawings and specifications and/or a description of the work (Scope of Work). You will see later how the proposal to the Client may, in some cases, become a simple contract by the addition of some cautionary phrases - when you think the value of the contract does not justify a lot of paperwork. Small projects often have no more documentation than this one piece of paper. But this one piece is the **absolute irreducible minimum.**

A very basic Plan of Operation (POP) may simply be the proposal that you submit to your potential Client. For a renovation project, this could be a:
- list of the work to be performed (scope of work),
- a time for completion and
- a cost

Just writing the list (scope of work) tells you what sub-trades you will need; what work you can perform yourself; gives an outline of the material required and the cost of the actual work. The time schedule governs your overhead costs which are an important part of the total budget; it also dictates your cash-flow - when interim payments will be received and made.

Depending on who provides the design information (it may be an architect employed by the Client), you may simply state in your Plan of Operation that "plans and specifications are provided by ....".

also see Section 4, Documents,"Proposal" (pg. 157)
also see Section 3, "Scope of Work" (pg. 54)

EXECUTION

With a proper Plan of Operation (POP) (minimal though it may be) and good management, a successful project is inevitable .... well, *almost* inevitable.

Assuming the plan has been established in some format or other (but preferably **not** on the back of an envelope), then successful execution (or implementation) of the plan means first:

- a legal **agreement** with the Client
- **communication** with Client, Architect, Engineer, etc.
- **communicating** the Plan to the Sub-trades and workers
- **coordination** of the work and the workers
- **supervision** and inspection of the workmanship
- proper **"follow-up"** AND
- an attitude of **"accountability",** an acceptance of **total** responsibility, by the Project Manager or Builder

In respect of "communication", if they don't communicate with **you,** then you must communicate with **them.**

also see Section 3, Project Planning, "Plan of Operation" (pg. 39)

EVALUATION

Many of the subjects in this manual could themselves have a complete book written about them. Evaluation, that is the assessment of the logic of the project plan (POP) and of the success of the project, is one of them.

The Plan of Operation and especially the Logical Framework Analysis (LFA, a tabular planning format which will be introduced later) should provide all the basic information required to evaluate the success of the project. The information obtained during execution of the project, the data collected in the "project diary", is extremely valuable to every Project Manager (every Builder) and should be compiled not only with a view to compliance with cost, quality and schedule but to assist in the evaluation. Evaluation teaches something about a project, about both the planning and execution methodologies: it is useful to everyone.

Evaluation can be a complex subject and for now it can be ignored in its detail; but keep in mind the basic points that follow:

- establish success criteria during the planning stage (determine what conditions will tell you that the project is a success) - *this might be as simple as "I made a profit" but if that is all you have learned from the project, it will not be enough!*
- make sure the criteria are **measurable** - money or physical dimensions will do - not in a lot of detail but avoid a simple "feel-good" assessment;
- consider inspection and supervision as part of the evaluation exercise; so establish **staged** evaluation criteria that will tell you **how** the project is progressing **while** it is progressing - *this is actually easier than it sounds but, as an example - check how much you have spent when drywall is complete against how much you **estimated to** have spent at that stage; a queasy feeling in the pit of the stomach is not good enough*;
- a most important element of evaluation is the consideration of improvements; the next project should benefit from the failures of the last.

> All too often, valuable information is forgotten or lost; **keep a diary** and make written notes (in a **book** - not on scraps of paper stuffed in all your pockets). Make sure that you **learn from your mistakes** and from your successes. If it works well once it **may** work again. If it fails once, you can be **sure** it will fail again.

also see Section 3, Project Planning, ***"Schedule"*** *(pg. 48)*

SUMMARY

The following are the main elements that you have to consider in respect of planning for project management for builders:

FIRST STEPS

- a project plan considered in all the detail **appropriate to the size and importance of the project**; *you **already** make a plan - all I am suggesting is that you consider it in more detail and in a more structured format; the plan can **always** be improved - make it better, a little more detailed each time.*
- proper documentation to build from - drawings, specifications and contract
- a proper legal environment
    - a contract with the client
    - **written** agreements with your Subs - *these agreements may be Purchase Orders with some modifications - more on this later.*

DURING EXECUTION

- effective coordination of the workers or Sub-trades and suppliers
- regular, **thorough** supervision - *this probably means much more time than you **usually** spend on site, more time reviewing the drawings*
- maintenance of proper records - accounts, project diary
- a proper "attitude" on your part; a willing acceptance of full responsibility for the work that both you **and your sub-trades** produce
- communication - keep everyone aware of what is happening
- **written** approvals, when due, by authorities having jurisdiction over the work (Client, Architect, Engineer, Municipal Inspector, etc.)

AFTER "COMPLETION"

- a proper and objective willingness to put right what has gone wrong, promptly and thoroughly
- an evaluation based on what you **expected** to achieve and what you **actually** achieved
- a logical, unbiased appraisal of the success or failure of the project; this will be from financial, organizational and promotional viewpoints

> I cannot stress too strongly the negative effect of the Builder sloughing off responsibility onto the Sub-contractor that actually performed the work. The Client is entitled to deal with only one person - the Builder/Contractor. He or she doesn't want to hear that a certain Sub is responsible. **The Builder, must carry the can** for errors and omissions - they are controlled by the *Builder*.

DEFINITIONS FOR BUILDERS

A few project management terms that apply particularly to building/construction are given below. Many of these terms will not immediately concern the small builder but when the small builder becomes a large one, they will be important.

Back-charge a financial charge (debit) against the contract of a party controlled by the Builder usually for a failure to perform properly or for damage to another party's work

Bar Chart see Gantt Chart in "Project Management Definitions"

Builder	used interchangeably with "Contractor" in this book. See Contractor, below.
Change Order	an instruction from the Client or a Consultant (the Client's Agent) to modify the contract; usually results in a change to the price and/or duration of the project (also called Variation Order)
Clerk of Works	a specialist trade inspector usually employed by the Client or the Client's Agent or Consultant, or sometimes an "Authority Having Jurisdiction" over the project
Construction Management	means the *profession* of Construction Management. In other words, the employment by a Client of a manager or management company on a fixed or variable fee basis to conduct all the functions of the Client on behalf of the Client, employing individual contractors by direct contract between the Client and the Contractor
Contractor	this book employs the term as a builder of any type of construction; civil, mechanical, multi-use buildings, houses, renovations, additions, external works, etc.
Control	my definition is that "whoever controls the money, controls the project"; all contractual relationships in building, or anything else, are about money
General Contractor	the General Contractor is the Contractor who holds the contract with the Client whether it is for **all** of the work or **part** of the work. *It is possible for the Client to have more than one General Contractor on a project - but it is not a good idea unless they are separated geographically*
Hold-back	part of a due payment held back either by a Client from a Builder or a Builder from a Sub-contractor to compensate for potential non-payment of suppliers and workers; usually 10% and usually held for a specific period (37 to 45 days) by law
Interface	the point in either time or physical space where two activities or things meet; it may be both as, for instance, when one trade contractor follows another (time and space)

project management for Builders and Contractors

Lump Sum Allowance   a Prime Cost Sum - see below

Package   that part of a project that is tendered as a whole, although it is not the complete project. It is common in design/build projects when the extent and nature of the project is not fully known at the commencement of work; a "trade" contract is a package

Prime Cost Sum   an allowance (money) specified and contained in the contract price, to be expended against certain specific elements of the Work under the direction of the Client or the Client's Agent

Site Instruction   a written instruction to perform or clarify a task within the parameters of the contract. It may or not involve a change in the contract price. Properly issued by the Client or Consultant or Construction Manager but often by the Builder on behalf of the Client, carrying the confirmatory signature of the Client (or the Client's Agent)

Sub-Contractor   a Contractor who is directly employed by a General Contractor and who has no direct relationship with the General's Client.

Variation Order   a Change Order - see above

PROJECT MANAGEMENT DEFINITIONS

Some common terms used in more general project management are defined below. These are definitions based on both dictionary interpretations and experience of a majority of popular uses. Until recent efforts of the Project Management Institute (PMI), project management terminologies had not been sufficiently and so universally standardized that everyone could agree with them; however, as long as the terms are common within a project or a program, some variation is not important.

Action   anything done or performed but in project management terms usually a short-term and decisive action

Activity   in project management terms, usually describes a protracted action or series of related actions, differentiated from another series of actions within the same project *see Task, below*

Beneficiary	the person or persons or group that benefits from the project; may be either the Client or those that the Client represents
Client	essentially, the person, persons or institution that provides the money or the *motivation* that makes the project possible or otherwise benefits from the completion of the project; may be the Beneficiary (see above) or may be a department in a large company or government organization
Contract Package	see "Package" in "Definitions for Builders"
Critical Path	the **longest** path through a network of tasks that defines the duration of the project; *the path that the Project Manager has to worry about*
Duty	what is required to be done, a moral or legal obligation
Evaluation	appraisal in financial, organizational and strategic terms of the success of the project or program
Function	occupation, office, something performed or done
Functional Management	a management system for the control of multiple specialized activities on a long-term basis within an established organization
Gantt Chart	a simple bar chart in which elements of the project are shown starting and finishing on horizontal lines against a time schedule. It is the simplest chart for controlling implementation and is readily understood. It also assists in developing cash flow. *See Section 3, Project Planning, "Schedule"*
Goal	a broad, strategic objective to which the project contributes
Input	the requirement of service, finance and material that will produce the output
Logical Framework	a tabular format that relates cause to effect, considering all the factors that might affect the project or the long-term program

Matrix	a shape or form across a diversity of different functional units: in other words, a "Team" selected from a variety of functional departments
Milestone	a significant point in the development of a project whereat an intermediate conclusion may be reached and a decision made
Network Diagram	see PERT below
Organization Chart	usually a chart showing the relationship between people or authorities within an organization and/or peripheral to the organization that might affect it
Organigram	a term, used in this book, for Organization Chart
Output	the product resulting from the application of the inputs during the execution of the project
PERT	**p**rogram **e**valuation and **r**eview **t**echnique; a network planning tool relating tasks to each other on the basis of time and precedence and producing a *critical path* through the project (see "Critical Path")
Plan of Operation	the project plan or framework that tells you how to implement or execute the project and how to benefit from its execution
Procedures	all the information required to use the system effectively
Program	usually a series of associated or complementary projects all having the same "goal" within an overall financial and organizational structure
Project	a project exists as a "task" entity but not as an administrative entity; this is, of course, in the context of matrix management: it has a beginning and an end (the PMI defines project as "a temporary process undertaken to create one or a few units of a unique product or service whose attributes are progressively elaborated"): *for the small builder a project is obviously a "job" and includes the **planning** of the job*

Project Management	the Project Management Institute (PMI) says that project management is the "management of change" as distinct from "general", "operational" or "technical" management: it is **not** PERT or CPM or any other mechanism.; *"change" for the builder amounts to going from seeing nothing to seeing a completed building or structure - obviously, it has to be properly managed*
Purpose	the end objective of the project
Responsibility	the condition of accepting moral and legal accountability for one's actions
Results	are the product of the "outputs" of a project and the behaviourial changes that those new outputs induce in the users of the outputs *(see my book "**incredibly easy project management**" for details)*
Role	a function or act or series of functions or acts that one is required to perform
Task	usually a series of activities that form a whole within a greater whole, usually within a project
Team	all those engaged on the project under the control or influence of the Project Manager

*It is not essential to memorize **all** these terms. They are here when you need them..*

BUSINESS PROMOTION

Because this book is not about sales methods nor advertising, nor promotion, it only refers briefly to this important aspect of a builder's work and assumes that you already have a project or projects and have done what you should do to obtain more work. The primary element of promotion is, in any case, having a worthwhile service to sell. If you perform well, if your projects are successful, if you make enough money to stay in business, then you have the best sales pitch available - **client referral**.

Carefully do the things recommended and improve on them for each new project and you will be sure of further projects. (Remember "attitude" and "precision"). But one thing that is important, no matter how effective your planning and management techniques, is **presentation.** This book contains sample documents to submit to your Client. A neatly printed proposal, a well drawn plan, a well-considered contract, convince the Client that you are a responsible person or company, that you are neat and tidy in your work and that you are sufficiently concerned to make a good impression. This is more striking in the small builder than the big enterprise. In the latter - it is expected. For the small contractor, it puts you one up on your competition.

BUSINESS AND CONSTRUCTION NOTE

A wealthy American banker was building a huge house on a Caribbean island. His builder was short of capital and it was generally known that his cash-flow was precarious. The Owner drove a hard bargain and the Builder, desperate for another project to keep him going, knowingly underestimated. The Owner was a smart businessman and set himself up on a hill overlooking the building site with a pair of binoculars (and a shaker of martinis) to make sure that all the materials he was paying for (materials on site) were actually delivered. Each and every day he watched truck-loads of Honduras Mahogany, sand and cement, re-bar and so on delivered to the site. Satisfied, he retired to his hotel at night for a couple more martinis and commenced his vigil the next morning. If he had looked closely he may have seen the cloud of dust left by the trucks that spent all night removing the materials to a number of other building sites!

CONSTRUCTION NOTE

The house, on a Jamaican beach, was recently finished with a cedar shake roof on laths, on hand-cut trusses, open to the rooms below. The Owner complained of a tapping and scraping noise in the roof, usually early in the morning. Our roofers carefully investigated the ridge - nothing. The noises continued. The mechanical contractor checked the flashings at his roof penetrations - all in order. The noises continued. I sent the electrician to determine if there were any loose wires in the trusses. Still no solution. To appease a very irritated Client, I ventured out at dawn and sat on the beach to watch. Before long a flurry of wings heralded the problem but not, I am afraid, a solution. Four vultures landed on the roof ridge and set to cleaning their beaks on the edges of the shakes. In Jamaica they are a protected species. Perhaps they are still there every morning. How about that for an unforseen overhead cost?

SECTION 2

SOME DETAIL

PLANNING

Two aspects of planning were touched on in Section 1, **Strategic** Planning and **Project** Planning. As a Project Manager, you are more concerned with *Project* Planning because that is where the most vicious alligators are. As a business-person, you must give some consideration to Strategic Planning because it concerns all your projects and it also concerns all your money. Some more detail follows.

STRATEGIC PLAN

In the Introduction I said that planning is the stage at which a project may be most easily undermined and that good planning is the foundation-stone of good execution. This was in reference to **project** planning but is equally true of **strategic** planning. What, you may ask, is strategic planning?

In the simplest terms - and the principle really **is** a simple one - it is **planning for the long term**. To make use of a couple of the terms introduced earlier, it is planning mostly in terms of "Goal" and "Purpose".

Don't get up-tight about this subject (not yet); it will become clearer as we consider planning in general. We are really talking about good business sense.

So what is your "Goal" as a builder? The next chart shows (starting from the bottom) that your Inputs produce an Output; your Output (what you produce) is a final stage in achieving the Purpose of the project and the Purpose (why you are producing it) is one part of your overall long-term Goal. You will have many projects; therefore many Purposes - all of which go towards the achievement of the Goal. Both Purpose and Goal may be considered strategic aims within your strategic plan. Inputs and Outputs are the principal considerations in your **project plan or Plan of Operation (POP)**.

STRATEGIC PLAN	Goal	
	Purpose	⇑ eventually & accumulatively achieves the Goal
PROJECT PLAN	Output	⇑ outputs lead to the Purpose
	Inputs	⇑ inputs, properly utilized give the Output

Goal

Your long-term Goal (considered within your strategic plan) may be *"to retire at fifty with a villa in Spain"* or *"to produce excellent products that will provide income security and early retirement"*. They both mean pretty much the same thing but the second one displays a better **attitude.** Producing an excellent product is important to the builder who expects to serve an expanding clientele and deciding how to ensure you provide that product is part of your **strategic plan.**

The *Goal* is your long-term objective
- own your own golf course, perhaps?

Except for medium-to-large companies with multiple projects and staff who need to be informed of company policy, there is no absolute need to produce a **document** labelled as "Strategic Plan". It is sufficient to have the thought, the idea of what you intend to achieve in the long term. However, committing it to paper will keep it more certainly in your thoughts. This thought should motivate your every action. It should shape your business "style", govern the way you treat your Clients and your sub-contractors. It is worth mentioning that if you want a loan from the bank, they will ask for a business plan and your long-term strategy will suddenly become important - you will need some measurable milestones and some achievable financial targets.

Your bank will ask for a "business plan" - a Strategic Plan

If your company employs staff (superintendents, project managers, inspectors, planners, designers, etc.) a documented strategy is essential. If everyone knows the end goal, they can all adjust their working philosophy and habits to that goal. This is of much greater importance to the Project Manager than upper management generally appreciates; it encourages "team-work" and cooperation.

Purpose

"Purpose" is the immediate end objective of every **project.** In terms of the Strategic Plan, it may change as you obtain more projects. If you think it may change as you grow stronger and expand your business, then the Strategic Plan (mental plan or written plan) should show the change.

Initially, a Purpose, as you commence your business as a Builder, may be *"to establish a reputation for excellent but reasonably-priced work"*. A next Purpose - say after 3 years of successful business - may change to *"to maintain a reputation for good workmanship while accumulating capital for expansion"*.

At the risk of over-simplification and repetition, the implication here is that you believe that making a profit in the early days is not so important as doing good work in order to establish a reputation. As you expand, your efficiency will improve and you may be able to increase your profit margin, allowing an accumulation of funds with which to expand the business.

The *Purpose* is what your completed project (building) will achieve for you

You probably already **think** in these terms. A Strategic Plan is merely the **format** into which you fit your thoughts. An example is shown very simply in the chart below with the sequence moving upwards through all the stages of achievement from Inputs to Goal. Inputs and Outputs will change with each project but Purpose and Goal remain the same until you modify your Strategic Plan. *It is, however, likely that in the normal development of a business, your Purpose will change more frequently than your Goal.*

STRATEGIC PLAN ELEMENTS

		DESCRIPTION
Strategic	GOAL	To produce excellent products that will provide income security and early retirement
	PURPOSE	Establish a reputation for excellent but reasonably-priced work
Project	OUTPUTS	Varies with each project - usually a building, an addition, a renovation
	INPUTS	Varies with each project (money, materials, labour, supervision, etc.)

STRATEGIC PLAN OUTLINE

If you wisely decide that you need a strategic plan and if you, equally wisely, wish to formalize it in order to guide your business development and plot your progress, there are some basics that you must consider. When establishing a new business, include, at least, all the items listed below. If you find that you do not achieve all your targets, if you fall behind in your schedule of implementation of the Plan, either decide that your plan is too ambitious and amend it or increase your efforts to achieve the targets. The choice is yours. But, at least, you will have a guideline against which to measure your achievements. Without guidelines you are flying by the seat-of-the-pants; never knowing where your business stands. You may be lucky but you may not.

Strategic Plan

Goal
    Objectives - Summary
    Financial Guidelines/Parameters
    Organization
    Personnel
Implementation Program
Budget
    Five-year budget
    Company Set-up
        Registration
        Licences
        Premises

Budget (contd)
    Equipment
    Office
    Construction
    One-year budget
    Income
    Cash-flow Diagram
Promotion - Methods
Standard Documents
    Proposal
    Contract
    Purchase Order

PLAN OF OPERATION - PROJECT PLAN

The project plan is usually referred to as the Plan of Operation **(POP).** It should be designed to answer all the questions that might arise during the planning, execution and evaluation of a project.

    The amount of information and the amount of detail required for the POP is always dependent on the peculiarities of the project. No two projects are identical even if they only differ in cost - so, identical POPs are the exception rather than the rule. Their similarities lie in the fact that each POP requires specific answers to certain questions; the information contained in the response is the variable.

    Even where a minimal POP is being employed (the back-of-the-envelope technique) or where the project is being run by the "seat-of-the-pants" method, some sort of order is required and certain factors have to be considered, certain questions relative to the success of the project must be asked. You certainly do this now but do you do it in a methodical manner?

The Plan of Operation gives the answers to the same basic questions that you must ask and answer for each project

Please accept that POPs for all projects must answer the same basic questions. The important questions are listed below; they should be answered in the section of the POP indicated but, if the POP is very rudimentary, just answer them wherever you think fit - but **do** answer them.

QUESTION	ANSWER -included in:
What will the project produce?	Logical Framework (LFA) - Outputs; Description
Why is it required?	Background; LFA
Who will perform the work?	Organigram ; Activity Responsibility Matrix
How will the work be done?	Organization & Control; Organigram; Activity Schedule; Responsibilities; LFA
When will it start and finish?	Schedule; Activity Network;
How much will it cost?	Budget; Cash-flow; LFA, WBS
Where will it be done?	Location(s)
What can go wrong?	LFA; Special Considerations

*You have not yet met the **LFA** (Logical Framework Analysis) and you may never use it but it does provide a lot of information in very little space.*

Consider these questions when beginning to plan the project. Do not be put off by the planning terms or the seemingly tedious procedure. *You **must** be able to answer all these questions **now** - you are almost certainly doing so already - **one way or another**.* But it is important to know **why** you are asking and answering them, to get them in logical order and to have them in a recorded, standard format. You will see that most of the answers are contained in the **Organigram** (organization chart), the **Schedule** and the **LFA**. Make sure you have considered the answers before ordering materials, putting a spade in the ground - indeed **before signing a contract** with the Client. As an example of the importance of these questions and their relevance .... you may ask what importance should be attached to **"Where"** - the project location?

The answer is simple enough and could be very important cost-wise:
- geographically, it may be far from your headquarters - *extra transport*
- it may not have a water supply - *water storage on site and transport to site*
- you may be remote from your usual suppliers - *new, perhaps unreliable suppliers*
- your regular Subs may not want to travel so far - *risk of unknown Subs*

project management for Builders and Contractors 33

- there may be a surcharge for delivery - *additional cost*
  In terms of the site itself,
- it may be off-road - *build temporary road*
- perhaps it has a steep driveway - *parking problems, run-off from site with clean-up problems*
- if it is in a city, you may have to spend more money for access - *barriers, elevated office*
- you may suspect that the sub-soil in that area is not stable - *delays for testing*
- if it is remote from town, inspectors may delay their visits - *more delays*

Normally, your subconscious works out the answers to all these things for you (that is your Plan) but a little help from your conscious mind and a written list of the problems will improve your Plan.

Those three (Organigram, Schedule, LFA) are the key elements of the POP, especially the LFA - Logical Framework Approach (also called the Logical Framework Analysis). For the small builder they may be the complete POP. *An example of an LFA is given in an appendix to this book describing this special planning procedure.* For now, just consider the basics as they have been described.

The important planning (LFA) terms have been described above. Accept that, as a builder and a Project Manager, you are concerned principally with **Input** and **Output.**

As a businessman/woman (and all builders are business people), Goal and Purpose will also mean something .... but more of that later. The important point when planning a project is **"to know the answer to those questions above"**.

Without any doubt, you *need* a Plan of Operation!

A simple Plan of Operation will have or will refer to these sections:

- Budget and Cash-flow
- Logical Framework Analysis (LFA)
- Organigram (Organization Chart)
- Schedule
- Work Breakdown Structure (WBS)
- Scope of Work
- Agreement (Contract Format)

also see Section 3, "Project Planning" and Appendix "LFA" (pgs. 39 & 168)

CONTROL

The Organigram (Organization Chart) shows how the project will be **controlled,** how it will be managed. In the simplest form of contract, the General Contractor employs several sub-contractors. So, you already know that you are "in charge", that you have the theoretical authority - but this is often different to being in "control". You have to make sure that you don't lose **control** during the execution of the project. **The elements of control are established during the *planning* process.**

The fundamental key to control is control of the money. This depends first on your contract with the Client, then on your contracts with your Sub-contractors, your agreements with your suppliers and ultimately on how you manage those contracts. The contracts establish the project cost and the basis of payments; normal contract formats and procedures ensure that the project is "controllable". The extension of this is how skilfully, during execution of the project, you control the money both in convincing the Client to pass it along to you and in not passing along more than is legally and effectively due to anyone else.

When you sign a contract with the Client, he/she theoretically passes **control** to you, the Builder. Obviously, as long as the Client retains control of payments, he or she keeps control of the project. When the money control is passed to you by the Client (through a disbursement), you have to exercise extreme care in disbursing those funds. Do not overpay. If the lien laws require a hold-back by the Client on payments to the General Contractor or if it is otherwise a term of the Client/Contractor Agreement, then hold back a similar amount from your Subs.

To make this possible, you must have a very clear idea of your payment schedule for all your Subs - which is an essential part of your planning. This tight payment policy may give you a bit of trouble but try to establish it gradually as a business principle. At the same time, be fair. If the work has been done satisfactorily and a payment is due, pay it! Similarly for your agreement with your suppliers; it is important to schedule your purchase of materials to suit your receipts from the Client. If they extend credit, make sure you meet your bills on time or supplies may be cut off. All of which implies the need for a clear construction and payment schedule.

Whoever controls the money controls the project

In Section 3 of this manual I shall explain why it is often better to ask the Client to make smaller payments more frequently and why you should pass along these payments to your Sub-contractors on a similar basis.

also see Section 3 "Schedule" (pg. 48)

PROJECT EXECUTION

Execution/implementation is the fact of putting the plans into effect, setting out the structure, and starting to build. Execution may be considered as completed when the final payment has been made and the structure handed over. (Do not forget the maintenance period; this should be thought of as part of the project and should have a cost assigned to it).
Execution will be considered now under:

- **Coordination**
- **Supervision**
- **Follow-up**

COORDINATION

Getting everyone and everything to the project site at the right time, in the right order and without everyone tripping over everyone else is probably what a builder does best. If you are not having reasonable success in this task already, then you are in deep trouble. However, proper planning can make the task easier.

A BAR CHART ASSISTS COORDINATION

A bar chart (Gantt chart) showing the relationships between the trade contractors will make the job easier. It is not a big deal. If you don't find it easy to prepare such a chart, then you probably are not coordinating the work as well as you should. The logic of one trade following another is fundamental to construction practice and, if you can do it, you should be able to draw it! A sample chart that shows the **principles** you should adopt is given in Section 3, "Schedule". Any delay or confusion in getting your Subs or workers to the job means an extension of building time and this means an increase in your overheads. **Their** time is **your** money.

also see Section 3 " Schedule" (pg. 48)

SUPERVISION

Most Builders do not spend enough time on supervision or inspection. One-person businesses, even when employing Sub-contractors, are probably on the site often enough to make sure that everything goes well. Small to medium-sized builders have the greatest problem. Perhaps not big enough to employ a supervisor but too big to do all the supervision personally. Some large builders are also delinquent in this respect. Leaving a Sub to work alone in the knowledge or hope that he/she will remedy his/her errors later is not good enough. This always means delay, may delay a following Sub-trade and usually involves unnecessary paperwork. **Failure to supervise adequately always costs the General Contractor (Builder) money.**

As a small builder you may, of course, solve this problem by working twice as hard yourself. You may have to work a lot harder going through the transition from small to large but if you don't supervise properly, the work will be badly done, you will not get referrals and you may never get to be a big contractor anyway. Thinking ahead, planning properly and coordinating properly will make the supervision easier. But it still means a lot of hard work, a lot of time on the project. Employ a part-time inspector if you must. **Do not neglect supervision.**

> If you *prefer* to make excuses to the Client for a dining room light fixture that doesn't hang in the right place rather than make sure, during construction, that it *does,* then this book won't help you.

also see Section 3, "Supervision" (pg. 89)

PROJECT COMPLETION

When the whole thing has been built, the Project Manager does not just walk off the job and go on to the next project. No matter whether the project is large or small, the function of the Project Manager is to assure him/herself that everything is going to work, that all the legal matters have been taken care of, that payments have been made, warranties and guarantees initiated, insurances terminated and, of course, the Client has been made completely happy. This subject is dealt with more completely in Section 3, but take note of the bare essentials. The Project Manager must:

- test all equipment to ensure proper function - this means **everything**; on a small project, turn on the taps, flush the W.C.; on a large project, run the central air-conditioning, check laboratory exhaust systems, operate furnaces, test emergency generators, and so on
- consolidate all site instructions and change orders to verify the final cost
- Complete and obtain approval of "as-built" documents
- make final inspections with concerned parties
- correct deficiencies and complete unfinished work

also see Section 3, "Project Completion" (pg. 118)

FOLLOW-UP

Follow-up **during** project implementation means leaving nothing to chance or to the goodwill of others. Make sure you do the following:

- follow up **in writing** on any changes to agreements made during project implementation with Client, with Sub-contractors, with anyone involved in the success of the project
- follow up ahead of time - **anticipate;** that is, make sure that you remind people in advance that they are supposed to be somewhere or provide something or complete a task at a certain time. You may irritate someone but you will get things done on time and you will have a better idea of what is happening and so .... better coordination
- follow up on remedial work; make sure that your Subs or staff have done what they said they would. Don't wait for the Client or another Sub-contractor to complain that something has not happened, that the work is being delayed
- follow up on things that are not supposed to happen. If there is an unavoidable delay, make sure that everyone concerned knows about it. This is an important element of communication and is often neglected. It is not fair, nor is it good business, to have people turn up on the site if some element for which you or another Sub is responsible is not in place or not completed or poorly performed. It could cost you money - **communicate!**

EVALUATION

PROJECT EVALUATION

If you have made a lot of money (or maybe if you just haven't **lost** any money) when the building, addition, or renovation is completed, and the Client is not mad at you, you may assume that the project was a success. That is the simplest form of evaluation. However, it is not likely to be that easy. In the first place, there is the warranty period to be completed - so completing the construction, is not the same as completing the **project.** Many builders assume that they can pay for anything that goes wrong out of the next project's cash-flow. This may not be a conscious **plan** but it certainly happens in fact.

But this casual appraisal is not good enough if you wish to benefit from your mistakes and if you want to improve your performance on the next project. It is necessary to review the project from the financial, organizational and promotional viewpoints. This will be nearly impossible unless you started with a Plan (POP). For the time being, just be aware that this relationship between project planning and evaluation exists. When we get around to the details of the LFA you will see how it can be simplified.

STRATEGIC EVALUATION

How often is it necessary to review and evaluate the Strategic Plan?

Perhaps you lie in bed at night worrying about the progress of your business. In effect, you are reviewing or evaluating your Strategic Plan. Not the best way to do it but it is an indication of how important long-term goals are in justifying your everyday activities.

When you have a written plan, a 3-year review is probably sufficient. If your business makes unexpected gains or if you suffer unexpected reverses, then you should look at your long-term plans immediately. A certain amount of common-sense is required. It may be enough to conclude in a general way that your plan is a good one if all of the following conditions apply:

- you feel good about your business
- you have a positive bank balance
- you have repeat business from the same Clients and
- you keep getting new clients.

However, in the same way that **measurable** targets are recommended for a project in order to simplify evaluation, so there should be **measurable** targets in the strategic plan. An annual volume of business yielding a certain percentage profit would be one method. For instance *"annual turnover of $1 million in year three, yielding 4% net profit"*. If your turnover is substantially less at the end of year three, you will know by how much you missed the target and try to determine what went wrong - assuming, of course, that the target was realistic in the first place.

There are many other factors that you could consider such as: number of employees; capital investment in properties built; undeveloped land holdings; that villa in Spain, and so on. Remember that if your bank is providing financing they will want to see your long term business plan and will check it periodically against your current progress to ensure that their money is safe.

CONSTRUCTION NOTE

In the 1960s, residential construction in Jamaica, mostly of concrete block and ring beams, had to be earthquake proof. It was required that re-bar be continuous from foundation to ring-beam. So masons were required to lift each block to the height of the beam and drop it down over the reinforcing steel. No dowels were permitted!

SECTION 3

MORE DETAIL

The previous pages have covered in outline, the **basic** elements of project Planning, Implementation/Execution and Evaluation. Section 3 considers them in more detail and also looks at the need for and the type of documentation required to control your projects and to keep you out of trouble.

PROJECT PLANNING

PLAN OF OPERATION (POP)

The Plan of Operation or POP is always your basic planning document. If you are still in the "back-of-the-envelope" mode, if you still rely on those old cigarette packages stuffed into your pockets or out in the pick-up, then **that** is your POP (not recommended, mind you). Whatever bits and pieces of information and calculations you have assembled for a project become the POP.

Obviously, the more detailed and the better organized they are, the better the POP. So we shall look at some of the basic requirements; in roughly the best order of importance. Some of them may seem, at first, a bit weird or unnecessary but you can give more importance to those that seem most relevant to you for the project you are working on. Once you get into an orderly frame of mind, you will begin to understand your needs better and can add to or rationalize your POP for future projects.

The outline POP below is for a fairly complex plan of operation for a large project, not necessarily a building project (remember that the **principles** of project management are universal). It gives you an idea of the amount of information that may be required for a complete and detailed plan. The elements that are of immediate interest to you, the Builder, are indicated in bold italics. As your projects increase in size and value, if you get into property development, as your risks increase, so the other elements become more important and your Plans of Operation adjust to insure against the difficulties that may be encountered.

Plan of Operation

Contents
Table of Contents
Appendices
Abbreviations
INTRODUCTION
Background
Special Considerations
Logical Framework Analysis
Objectives **
DESCRIPTION OF THE PROJECT
Location
General Description
Project Design Strategy
Financial Parameters
Budget
Source of funds
Cost control
ORGANIZATION AND CONTROL
Organigram (Organization Chart)
Responsibilities and Roles
  Client
  Staff
  Consultants
  Associated Organizations
  Beneficiaries

Reports
Charts and Diagrams
Activity/Responsibility Matrix
Financial Procedures
Approvals Procedure
Payment Methodology
Monitoring Schedule
Implementation Schedule(Gantt chart)
Reporting Schedule
Detailed Budget and Cash-flow
Financial Approval Authorities
Approval Parameters
  Consultants
  Contractors
  Design
  Evaluation
Termination/Commissioning Parameters

APPENDICES
Contracts
  Consultant
  Contractor
Financial Agreements
Mortgage Format

    The bold, italicized items have more importance than most of the others to the small or one-person enterprise. They are **essential** to all Project Managers. The larger your company, the more important will the other items become. Keep in mind that "Objectives"(** **see above**) which would include your "Purpose" and your "Goal", could influence decisions that are made throughout the implementation of the project.

    For instance, if one of the key "objectives" or the **Purpose** is to establish the construction company in a new area, you might decide to trim your profit margin; you might even (unthinkable thought) decide to take a loss on the first of several units in order to become established. This may be a decision to be refined and acted on by the Project Manager in the field. The "objective", the conditions governing it, its financial parameters, would have to be established in the POP. Tight control of such a situation is essential to avoid a planned reduction in profit margin becoming an unanticipated loss. For which reason clarity and communication are all important.

Some other items of the POP have importance as background to all your project management and construction activities - part of your **strategy** which affects your project.

A one-person enterprise will have these considerations in the back of the mind as decisions are being made. A large company with subordinate staff making similar decisions needs an established policy, in writing, for each project so that the proper determination can be made in the proper context by the person in charge. This established policy should be derived from the strategic plan. So we can say that the bigger the organization, and the bigger the project, the more important a complete POP becomes - taking for granted that a strategy exists.

The elements that will tell everyone the most about the project are:
- **B**udget and **W**ork **B**reakdown **S**tructure - used in making your estimate
- LFA (Logical Framework Analysis)
- Organigram (Organization Chart)
- Schedule of Implementation
- Contract Documents containing:
    * Plans and Specifications
    * Scope of Work
    * Agreement/Contract

These items alone, when expanded a little and coordinated with each other, can tell you most of what you need to know, in practical terms, of a small project. and will provide the fundamentals for a large project. A brief description first; then we shall see how they tie together.

BUDGET

The project **budget** may be considered as confirmed when an estimate is approved and accepted by the Client. The Builder or the Builder's estimator has calculated certain costs for time, material, overhead and profit. If the client accepts the total, then that is the project budget. The Client may have a slightly different, hidden figure in mind; might, in fact, have a personal budget that is larger than the contracted price because he/she anticipates the possibility of additional work as the project progresses (sometimes the Client may have a smaller budget planned, expecting to cut costs as the project proceeds!). In effect, there is the client's budget and the **Builder's budget**.

The latter is of immediate importance. If you knew what the Client had in mind for a total budget it might influence your bidding - but that doesn't happen often. There are many estimating methods which vary with the type and size of project. This book will consider the Work Breakdown Structure (WBS) as the most useful one for builders and the one which most closely follows standard building procedures and standard estimating methods.

Builders who are also developers (small or large) will be both Client and Contractor. Probably a different department will create the budget or it may come from the Board of Directors through General Management to the Operations Department. In this case, of course, the Board is the Client and the Operations Department is the Builder. Essentially, **there is no difference in relationship to that of an external Client**; except that the same-company Client may be more demanding and harder to get along with.

This relationship within a company or a bureaucracy is important. It is to the advantage of all the parties that the relationships be clearly spelled out; that clear lines of **control** be established. Without this very basic requirement, you can guarantee conflict and bickering. The **project** is always more important than the existing hierarchy and other peoples sensibilities.

> A government agency was undertaking an overseas program for which the Department of Transport would be the "executing agency". The Project Officer in charge asked my advice on the Terms of Reference. I wrote them out in some detail, calling for a reporting and approval procedure that would maintain the control where it should be - with the source of the funding. The terms I recommended were considered too "harsh" and were watered down to allow more control to the executing agency, perhaps because of a "seniority" perception. Largely because of the split in "authority", the project was over budget and substantially behind schedule within the first two years.

also see Section 3, "Work Breakdown Structure" & "Estimating" (pgs. 73 & 66)

LOGICAL FRAMEWORK ANALYSIS (LFA)

This planning format must be mentioned, again only briefly, because it can be especially useful when your business has grown, when you are considering expansion or if there is a complex project in which you have a financial interest; in these circumstances especially, it could be considered essential. But, if you have the time and the inclination and you really want to understand the implications of a proposed project, the LFA will give you an answer for even the smallest project. It will make you **think** about the implications of what you are doing, what are the problems you may run into and what you can do to anticipate and minimize them.

If you don't feel like reading this, skip to the next sub-heading & see Appendix 1.

project management for Builders and Contractors

Essentially the LFA comprises 4 vertical columns which provide information about the four horizontal rows of Inputs, Outputs, Purpose and Goal as shown below.

Figure 2

NARRATIVE SUMMARY	OBJECTIVELY VERIFIABLE INDICATORS	MEANS OF VERIFICATION	IMPORTANT ASSUMPTIONS
GOAL			
PURPOSE			
OUTPUTS 3-bed, 200 sq.mt. house	Completed house valued at $400,000	Architect's final certificate	Schedule allows closing-in by Nov. 30
INPUTS			

In the first column (Narrative Summary) there will be a brief description of each level *(see Strategic Plan on page 27)*. As an example an Output could be: "*3-bedroom 200 square meter house*". "Objectively Verifiable Indicators" (OVI) in Column 2 simply means the things you are able to measure. For instance, at level 2 (progressing from the bottom up), Outputs might be *"house valued at $400,000"*. "Means of Verification" refers to how you would recognize the Input, Output, etc. In the case of Outputs, for a Builder, it might be *"Architect's final Certificate"* (that means the project is finished and recognized as such by the "authority").

You might think it all a bit remote from every-day operations. But consider the fourth column, "Important Assumptions". Essentially, these are all the things at each level that you forecast might, at that level, affect the outcome of the project. In fact, you may consider it as all the things that can go wrong. For instance, an "Important Assumption" when building anything in whatever locale in whatever country, is that the weather cooperate. A severe winter can involve additional heating if you wish to continue work. An uncertain water supply might have detrimental effects in a location remote from ready-mix concrete. So, one of the important assumption at level 2 (Outputs) might be *"that the schedule is maintained to allow closing in before November 30"*. If you have any reason to speculate (because, perhaps, of delayed approvals), before you actually start site work, that this will not happen, then you know you are in trouble. **There are generally several "important assumptions"(things to go wrong) at each level**.

Well, you may say, - you know all that anyway without the benefit of a chart.

But when you have it all written down, in each column at each level, you will be fully aware of the problems **all** the time, how problems at a lower level can impact on those at a higher level and what remedial action you may have to take. This may seem at first glance a painful methodology but it is what is required for a successful project and it gets a lot easier the more often you do it. What is more, everyone engaged on the project will be aware of the problem(s) and can anticipate what might be involved from their particular point of view. It is a "communication" tool.

also see Appendix 1, "LFA" and Section 2, Planning, "Strategic Plan" (pgs.168 & 28)

ORGANIGRAM - Organization Chart

If you are a one-man band (or a one-woman band) you may think an organization chart is not necessary. But it **is** because it tells you **graphically and simply** what human resources (sub-contractors, trades-people and staff - if you wish) you need for the project. If done properly, it makes you think about the project and reminds you, for instance, of whom you have to contact for quotations; it prevents major activities slipping through the cracks (the Work Breakdown Structure also helps in this regard). It also shows relationships with outside elements and, in that respect especially, assumes a significant contractual importance in that it shows who **controls** whom. For instance:

Figure 3

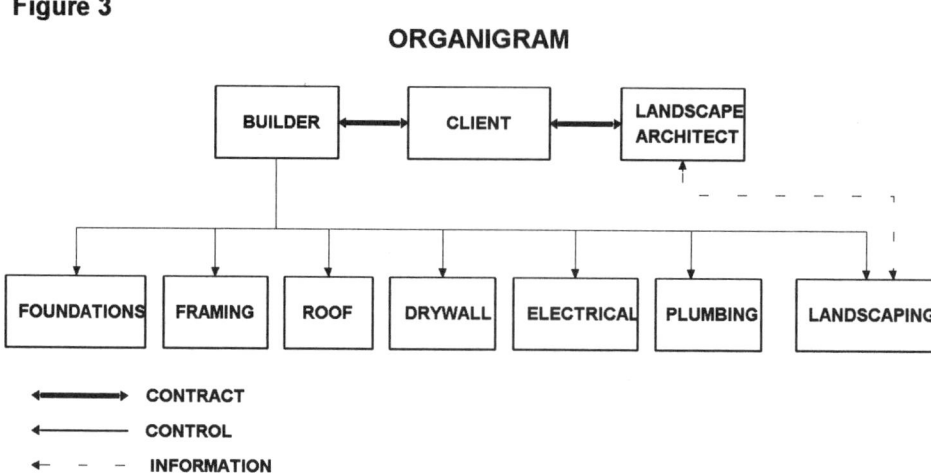

The above chart is so basic that it may not seem worth bothering with. But, consider the possibility of perhaps being unable to contract your

*usual foundation Sub-contractor. This may force you to split the foundation contract into several smaller units, contracting the formwork, reinforcing and stripping to two different Subs and placing the concrete by direct contract with a supplier and employing your own labour. Your chart now has 3 additional components. Instead of "Foundations" alone you would have "Formwork", "Re-bar", Concrete"). This could apply equally to any of the other building elements (tasks). This relates to your Work Breakdown Structure as you will see later and complicates both your estimating and, during implementation, your coordination - **more overhead costs**. The Organization Chart makes this obvious and makes it easy to react to changes before and during implementation/execution.*

The above chart clearly indicates a contract between the builder and the client (the thick line and double arrow-head). It also shows that the Client has an agreement with a Landscape Architect. There are **control** or authority lines from the Builder to all the sub-trades and there is a line of **communication or information** between the Landscape Architect and the Landscape Contractor. **This is an extremely important point** - it is an information/communication line and that is **all** it is.

Contractual obligations allow the Landscape Architect to **advise** the Client who can **instruct** the Builder who can, in turn, **instruct** the Landscape Contractor. Unless there is a specific clause in the Builder's contract to the contrary (and this would be very unusual), the Landscape Architect may **not**, repeat **not,** instruct the Landscape Contractor nor, for that matter, directly instruct the Builder.

Do not even **consider** having a clause in your contract that allows direct contact between a Consultant or Client and one of your Sub-contractors.

All the Builder's Sub-contractors and the Client should have a copy of this chart as a supplement to the contract or purchase order or whatever form of agreement is used. You may never have considered doing this but ask yourself - why not? It doesn't require hours of study or research to show who does what and who reports to whom. There it is on a simple piece of paper; it may be hand drawn and photocopied: if it is pretty, so much the better but it is more important that it exist and, of course, that it be correct; put a date on it - it may change - will almost certainly change.

ORGANIGRAM AS A CONTRACT DOCUMENT

It is obvious from the contract but more immediately so from the chart (which shows that all the lines of control - the authority lines-lead from the Builder or General Contractor to the Sub-contractors); it is obvious that if the Landscape Architect gives a direct instruction to a sub-contractor, that is a violation of the terms of the contract. If the Sub-contractor complies with such an unauthorized instruction from a Client's Agent or Consultant, then the Sub is financially responsible for any damaging consequences that result from the action and may be back-charged accordingly.

If the Builder (General Contractor) is not regularly available or does not have a system in place to allow this type of communication to filter backwards from the Landscape Architect, through the Client, through the Builder to the Sub, then the **Builder** is at fault. We shall look briefly into formal instructions and back-charging later in Section 3, "Project Completion".

All instruction *channels* must be contractually authorized

The Builder **must** follow contractual procedures him/herself and **must** be willing and available to transmit instructions to Sub-contractors at all times. Please, please do not take the easy way out and say to the Architect or the Client "Why don't you tell that directly to the Sub-contractor". If it makes it **much** easier, then you **must** be there with the Architect when he/she is talking to the Sub. This sort of direct communication between the involved professionals (or the Client) and the Subs causes many more problems than it saves time - and it usually costs money. A slightly more complex organization chart illustrates the problem as it might occur for a larger establishment on a larger project with a few more bodies involved.

Figure 4

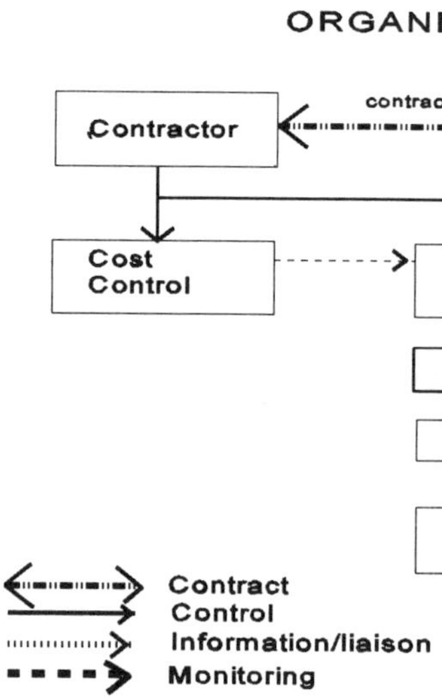

ORGANIZATION CHART

```
                    contract
   Contractor <═══════════════> Client
        │                         │
        ▼                         ▼
   Cost          Project              Designer
   Control ────> Manager  <────
                    │          │
                    ▼          │
                Secretary <────
                    │
                    ▼
                Supervisor <────
                    │              │
                    ▼              ▼
                 Project <■ ■ ■ Site Rep.
```

<═══> Contract
 ──>   Control
 ····> Information/liaison
 ■ ■ > Monitoring

In this example, should the inspection activities of the Site Representative (of the "Designer", who may be a landscape architect), disclose an error in implementation of the Work, s/he may bring it to the attention of the

project management for Builders and Contractors

Supervisor with whom there is an information or liaison relationship (the broken line). However, because this is only an "information/ liaison" relationship, the only legal or **contractual** recourse of the Site Representative in the event of **disagreement** with the Supervisor is to refer the matter back to the Designer, who controls or instructs the Site Rep.

The Designer, in turn, may **discuss** the matter with the Project Manager (another liaison/information relationship). But should no agreement be reached, then, for the same contractual reason, the designer **must** refer back to the Client who should resolve the dispute through the terms of the contract with the Contractor - it may involve a change and an "extra", for instance.

In general, although the contract is an agreement between two equal parties, the Client has the edge in any dispute because **the Client controls the money** - at least on the day that the contract is signed.

It follows that the Client should be expected to try to maintain this condition (control of the money) because the Client who overpays at any time during the life of the contract immediately loses absolute CONTROL at that point.

There is an enormous psychological (and financial) advantage to the Contractor who can induce the Client to pay beyond the value of work completed. At that point, the Client would feel inclined to view Contractor demands more favourably in the hope of persuading the Contractor to continue the work so that payments might eventually equal work completed.

For which reason, when the weight of contractual leverage is inherently on the side of the Client (a government department, for example) there is often a requirement imposed that the work be performed, without immediate recourse, on a written instruction when agreement cannot be reached on the value of a disputed item or action.

This invariably leads to in-fighting at the end of the contract; but it is usually accepted by the Contractor because of the other benefits of a contract with a government. But the point of this exercise is to show how useful is an Organization Chart (Organigram) in illustrating problems that might affect cost.

> The chart (Figure 3) on page 44 illustrates one of today's builders' major problems and major faults. The first page of this book refers to the proper "attitude" being the key to successful projects. One of the principal sins against attitude is allowing, even encouraging, direct **instructions** between different elements of the organization rather than passing information and instructions through the system. Quick **communication** is essential but **control and responsibility** are the obligations of the Builder, Contractor, Project Manager only (whatever title).

also see Section 3, "Control" (pg. 126)

Big Contractor or small, information must pass through the system

SCHEDULE

Obviously, the longer it takes to complete a project the greater the **overhead** and so, the greater the cost. Usually, both the Client and the Builder are anxious to complete the work as soon as possible. An implementation schedule is an important part of the Plan of Operation (POP) because it first indicates this significant cost element - "overhead" as it relates to the total duration of the project.

There are other considerations:
- availability of trade contractors - *you must know when your preferred contractors are available and line up substitutes just in case*
- coordination of trades - *because drywall follows rough electrical and plumbing, then you must give the drywall Sub a date on which to start work*
- scheduling of procurement (purchasing) affects cash-flow - *you don't want material on site that you can't integrate into the project immediately and when you need it, it has to be there; sometimes a Client will pay for "material on site" but not always*
- scheduling of payments - *the establishment of **milestones** in the schedule creates significant points in time and execution that suggest partial payment opportunities: e.g. on small projects - the completion of drywall installation before taping and filling could be a point at which an interim or progress payment may be justified from the Client and to the Sub.* **More detail on this later.**

It is rare to find a Client to whom time is not considered important. As outlined above, it is equally important to the contractor - if you don't know how long it will take, you **cannot** know how much it will cost - remember your overheads. Always develop a schedule of work for your own control purposes. It **should** form part of your contract; if you do not wish to commit yourself to the schedule in a legal sense, then refer to it as a "notional" or "anticipated" or "provisional" schedule. If it does nothing else, it shows that you have thought about the matter. If you are really doubtful of your ability to stick to even a "notional" schedule or of your ability to justify deviations from it, then better **not** include it in the contract.

Part of a typical bar-chart schedule is shown on page 49. It is not necessarily rational but it shows, for instance, several tasks that would be performed by an excavating contractor (clear site, mass excavation, foundation excavation); tasks to be performed by a framing contractor, an electrician, a plumber, a roofer and drywall contractor.

project management for Builders and Contractors

Figure 5

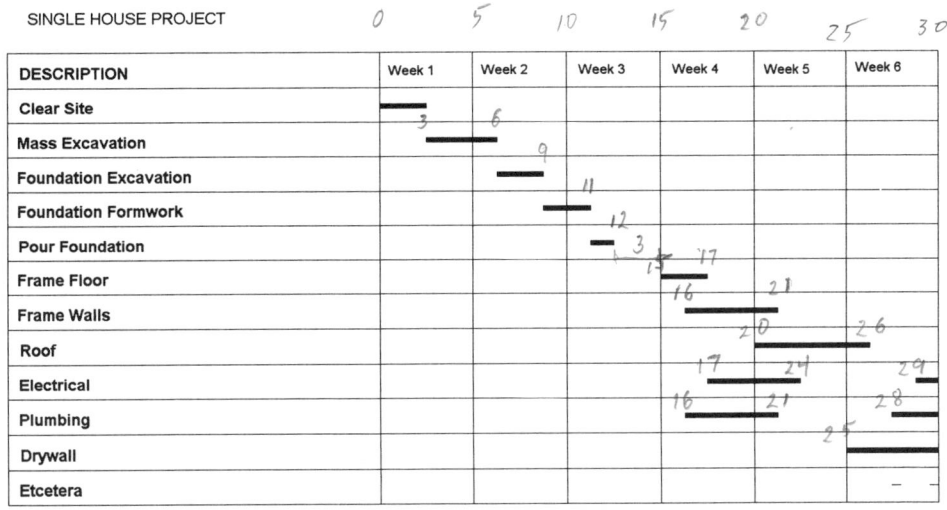

Because these *trades* appear in your schedule, it means that your Organigram must have corresponding Sub-contractors (or bodies) to perform this work.

Figure 3 (page 44) shows an organization that could generally correspond to this project schedule (**figure 5**), except that it ignores the "landscape" contractor whom we shall assume to be part of "etcetera" - along with cabinetry, finished carpentry, floor finishes, painting and so on. The schedule can be made clearer by joining the sequential operations with vertical lines to show interfaces of different trades; this is another step that assists in clarifying your thinking - it makes you more aware of the coordination that is required between the Sub-contractors and when it must occur (see **figure 6** on the next page).

SCHEDULE AND ORGANIGRAM COMPLEMENT EACH OTHER

In respect of time scheduling, you know which contractor follows which other contractor, that the electrician must begin roughing in while framing is in progress and must return later for "finish electrical." The Builder/Project Manager knows best the sequence of operations, which Sub-contractors are available and how long the work will take. Above all, a simple schedule such as this will tell you how long the project will take and how much of your time it will require - therefore what will be your overhead costs; and, ultimately, your profit.

"Overheads" are a major cost element

Figure 6

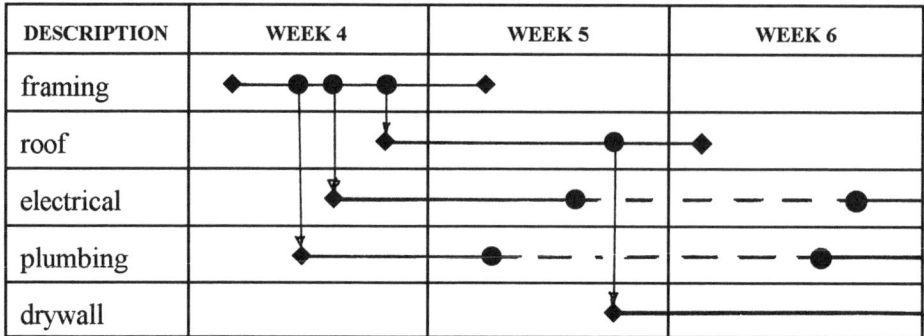

In **figure 6** a small section of the previous schedule **(Figure 5)** is enlarged to show connecting arrows between various trades. The vertical line from "framing" to "plumbing" indicates that the plumber commences roughing-in when about 25% of the framing is done. The next vertical line shows that electrical begins when framing is about 35% complete and so on; the roof commences when framing is about 80% complete (assuming in this example that there is some internal framing to complete). The drywall begins when the roof is about 85% finished.

The dotted lines tell you that electrical and plumbing are performed in two stages with the solid line indicating work time and the dotted line showing readiness to continue (finish electrical work may begin when drywall is under way).

In "electrical", for instance, the bar chart may show two, three or more sequences of operations - "roughing-in", "finish electrical" and "fixtures", for example. Depending on the duration of the project and the value of the work, this creates opportunities to make interim or stage payments to the Sub-contractors.

THE SCHEDULE AND STAGE PAYMENTS

The Project Manager may have agreed with the electrical Sub on values ($) for stages 1 and 2. When they are completed to the satisfaction of the PM, a stage payment less hold-back may be made. This anticipation and agreement to staged payments is preferable to the common alternative of having to respond to a Sub who says "How about an advance? - I am short of cash." Of course, this only works well when you have previously agreed corresponding interim payments from your Client that guarantee your cash-flow.

So one use of a schedule is to permit the determination of interim payments and to make it easy to consolidate them into advances to be paid by the Client. If you are asking your Client for frequent payments, the inclusion of the schedule as a "contract document" justifies these payments.

Why do this? Traditionally, builders and contractors have trouble with *cash-flow*. If you want to maintain good relationships with good Sub-contractors and have them prefer to work for you, ensuring that they are not starved for cash during the progress of the work is one way. Frequent, carefully calculated payments reduce their borrowing costs and so, potentially, their quotations to you.

On the other hand, it means that you have to **plan more carefully and monitor the work more carefully** to ensure that the work you are paying for is complete in all respects to the agreed stage. The example I chose (electrical) is probably the most difficult for the non-expert to measure; for instance, the simple omission of bushings or lock-nuts to conduit connections at all the outlet boxes could be a substantial cost element in respect of labour on a large project; if you don't notice that they are not there, you may be over-paying.

GANTT CHART

This type of bar chart is often called a Gantt Chart in which elements of the project are shown starting and finishing on horizontal lines against a time schedule. It is the simplest chart for controlling implementation of small to medium-sized projects and is readily understood by most people. It also assists in calculating cash flow.

Network Diagrams

The most common network diagram is the PERT (Program Evaluation and Review Technique) diagram which ties together all elements of the project defined in the Work Breakdown Structure (WBS) and provides a critical implementation path by determining which sequence of activities will take the longest time to perform. This is the **critical path** of the project. It is useful for large complex projects. In any case, without a computer, it is as well to avoid this method. If you have a computer program that performs PERT, it will be useful in those complex projects or for coordinating several **projects** within a **program** but its manipulation is better left to an expert in the technique.

CONTRACT DOCUMENTS

While I firmly believe that the Organigram and the Schedule should be included in any building contract, "contract documents" are usually thought of as plans and specifications, added to later where necessary by "shop drawings" and "as-built" drawings.

Some consideration of them follows in the order shown:

- plans and specifications
- scope of work
- acceptable legal contract format
- cost of the work
- shop drawings
- as-built drawings

(margin note: Contract Docs)

PLANS AND SPECIFICATIONS

Many small projects are performed (incredibly) without the benefit of plans and specifications. If there are documents, often they are inadequate, incomplete or just plain wrong. This is a major problem for a small builder because the Client usually does not appreciate the importance of proper documentation and is not prepared to pay the fee required to get the job done properly. *(Let me add, here, that it is unwise of a Builder to recommend a "drafting service", by name, to a Client - let the Client make any mistakes of choice, even of an Architect - and pay for the consequences).*

Whether the project is small or large, if there is documentation, the Builder should check it in detail; drawing against drawing and drawings against specifications. You are entitled, before bidding on a project, to ask for clarification of obscure design features or any other irregularity. In a competitive bid for a large project, the designer will issue addenda clarifying questions raised by the various builders who have been asked to tender.

This is not likely to happen on a small project and the Builder may simply irritate the Client by protesting the quality of the documents or pointing out errors. On the other hand, if you make a bid on the basis of faulty documents, you are in the difficult position of competing against other builders who may not have noticed the errors. This could mean that they bid lower than you because of inadequate checking or just plain ignorance of how things should be done. Of course, losing such a project could be a blessing in disguise.

Perhaps the best thing to do in such a case (for a small project) is simply to bid the project on the basis of what the designer submits as though it were correct. This is not easily done when your common-sense tells you that the design will not work but, unless it is a basically simple and obvious error, you are entering into the field of design yourself, potentially delaying the project, diminishing your own chances of a successful bid and getting up the Client's nose. Each case of documentation error must be approached in accordance with the circumstances. Your skill and experience will help you to decide for yourself.

However, if you decide to bid a suspect design, your first activity after being awarded the contract (that means a signed agreement), is to review the contract documents in great detail, note all the questionable features and ask either the Client or the Designer for a clarification. Do this **in writing** and indicate, at the same time, if you anticipate any increases or decreases in cost and increases or decreases in project duration. Don't forget - **do this in writing, immediately.** If there is a possibility of your having to make a claim for extras or if there may be a need to extend the contract, it increases your credibility and tends to legitimize your claims when you are on record at the earliest possible moment as having advised the Client - or his agent (in this case, the Designer). The question of claims for extras and changes will be considered later.

also see Section 3, "Changes & Instructions" (pg. 97)

In the case first mentioned of there being no drawings or specs, then your proposal, which contains your **scope of work** *(see Scope of Work, pg. 54)*, becomes the substitute for proper documentation. There must be some latitude in this document and the Client cannot or should not expect a detailed description that would totally replace drawings and specifications.

Should you, rashly, bid a substantial project on the basis of "sketch" or "outline drawings" only, using an educated assessment of square foot or square metre price, you are, in effect, offering to build a "complete" project (many houses are bid this way, perhaps with commercially printed sets of drawings). Interpretation of what is required, what is in fact "complete" could readily (almost certainly) lead to differences of opinion with the Client and potentially end in the courts.

Of course you want to avoid this, so your contract should contain a grandparent clause and you should have your lawyer check the contract before signing it. If you are dealing with such a situation, it follows that you will be providing the contract so you may insert in the Supplementary General Conditions something such as:

"The Work shall comply with the requirements of the National Building Code and the regulations of Authorities having Jurisdiction over the Work; shall be performed to the standards of the Central Mortgage and Housing Corporation and to the norms established by manufacturers and suppliers of materials and equipment to be incorporated into the Work and to the standards current for this type and category of construction in (...name the Country, State, Province, County or whatever is appropriate ....)". This is suitable for Canada (i.e.: CMHC). Change the names of the authorities and codes to suit the area in which the work is to be performed.

If a contract containing this clause were to come before a judge on a question of quality or omission, I submit that the judge would rule on the basis of what could reasonably be expected for the agreed price of the work; making comparisons with similar constructions in that area. A typical dispute may be that the Client thinks there should be a walkway all round the house and the Builder doesn't. If it is not shown on the drawings but other houses in the area have it - if, in fact, it is usually included whether shown or not - should it be included in the Builder's price? A Scope of Work solves or, at least, minimizes this problem (see "Scope of Work" below).

However, at the risk of repetition, if you are employing a lawyer to check your contracts (as you should - **always**), make sure that you and the lawyer are in agreement about the grandfather/mother/parent clause before you sign the contract.

SCOPE OF WORK - WORK DESCRIPTION

Proper contract documents will include not only plans and specifications but a "Scope of Work". This is a **general** description of what is required of the Builder or Contractor - or a **particular** description if there are no other documents. On a large project the Scope may be divided into sections that refer to trade activities. For smaller projects, it may not exist any more than do the plans and specs. As it is impossible for a builder to work successfully without this description, if it does not exist, then you, the Builder, must create it. Having said that it is impossible to work without it, nevertheless a good many builders do just that. Perhaps they are incredibly efficient or have a natural ability. Perhaps they even make money, but perhaps they have just been lucky.

As you prepare your estimate, of necessity you make a list of work to be performed and what each item costs *(see Work Breakdown Structure)*. The more detailed the list, the more accurate the estimate. The list is the basis for your Scope of Work and I recommend that it be submitted as your "proposal" to your Client. It makes clear what you intend to do for the contract cost. Individual item costs are not shown; just the items of work and the total cost of the project (for a "lump-sum" or "stipulated price" contract).

The danger in supplying this detail in a "proposal" to a new or unknown Client is that he/she may then take your Scope of Work and shop around to get a lower price using your Scope as a contract document. This is irritating in the extreme to the Builder. It cannot always be avoided. There are a couple of ways to handle the problem, but nothing totally satisfactory.

For a small project, you will just have to risk that the time you spend reviewing the work, preparing your estimate and writing the Scope is not wasted. Often, a good presentation, that is, a well-prepared and detailed Scope of Work will persuade the Client that you are a competent builder - that you know what you are doing. If there are several bids, this should give you an edge. Should the project require a lot of preliminary investigation, the recommendation of alternative methods, packaging for staged implementation, accumulative pricing, etc., then the Builder is, in fact, acting as a **consultant** and is entitled to a **fee** for this preliminary work. Explain to the Client that he or she is

THE BUILDER AS "CONSULTANT"

project management for Builders and Contractors 55

asking you to spend time (say two or three days) with no certainty of a contract for the work. Say that you are willing to prepare and submit a Scope of Work with an estimated cost for a minimal fee (name the amount and make it reasonable) which will be deducted from the project cost if awarded to you.

A Contractor is entitled to charge for an estimate or proposal that requires considerable investigation, analysis and recommendations of alternative methods

A reasonable person will see the justice of this. An unreasonable person will **not** and, in any case, would make a poor Client. Of course, it is important, if you suggest this procedure, to make a good presentation and to be thorough in your analysis and accurate in your pricing. If you cannot do this, maybe you should pass up the opportunity. But do not dismiss this "consultant" suggestion as an unlikely scenario. It has often worked in the past. If more builders adopt this procedure it will become more acceptable to the public. I promise you it will save you a lot of frustration and wasted time and, in the long run, save you money.

also see Section 3, "Contracts" & Section 3 "Estimating" (pgs. 91 & 66)

More on the Scope of Work

A Description of the Work may be in the form of drawings and specifications. As previously mentioned, often for the small contract (addition or renovation), there are either no drawings or they are found to be inadequate. So the written Scope (description) of Work is your basic document and you will probably, almost certainly, have to write it. The Work Breakdown Structure (WBS) will add to the usefulness of the Scope Of Work and make it easier to produce.

What does a Scope of Work do for **you** as builder or Project Manager?
It tells you:
- how many sub-trades you will need and what they are
- it suggests an order of work
- it ensures that you do no more than you have contracted for
- it establishes a basis for claims for additional work
- it establishes a schedule for ordering materials
- it gives an idea of how much time you must spend on coordination and inspection
- with the WBS it gives a sound basis for an estimate
- it shows interfaces with existing work and other contractors (if there are any)

What does it do for the **Client?**
- it leaves him or her in no doubt as to what he or she is getting for the money
- it eliminates arguments between Contractor and Client as to what was or was

not included
- ♦ it makes it easy for the Client to acknowledge a claim by the Contractor for extra money or time
- ♦ it saves the Client from that uncomfortable feeling that he/she is being bushwhacked

also see Section 3, "Work Breakdown Structure" (pg. 73)

Keep in mind, however, that even though the Client may read and seem to understand the Scope of Work, he or she may still **interpret** it differently from you, the Contractor. Which suggests that you cannot be too specific in describing the Work; it cannot be too detailed - at the same time, make sure it doesn't take longer to write the Scope of Work than it takes to perform the work.

A Scope of Work that stands alone without drawings and specifications must be comprehensive. It must indicate interfaces (junctions, unions, connections) between either materials, trades, other contractors or new work and existing. It must avoid including the scope of something beyond the interface but may refer to it for clarity only; it may have a grandmother/father clause or clauses that ensure(s) that, within the trade standards, there is no room for wriggling out of "normal" obligations; this catch-all is important where there are several different trades with somewhat similar expertise. For instance, if there is a junction of a plumbing fixture against an epoxy wall finish, who does the caulking? This may not be a problem for you but make sure it doesn't become one. Make sure that it is mentioned somewhere; if there are no specifications, put it into the Scope of Work.

As an example: *"All junctions between cabinet work and adjacent surfaces shall be caulked with an approved compound except where otherwise indicated in writing by the General Contractor".* The problem with this approach is that your scope of work now borders on a "specification" and you are assuming the role of "designer". However, it is only a small trespass beyond your role as Builder and you are probably aware that "caulking" is often neglected if not mentioned so, I believe it and similar cases are acceptable. You would be better off still with a specification.

All your Sub-contractors should have a copy of the Scope of Work; not in the form of the "proposal" that you submit to your Client because that gives your estimate - but the descriptive information. If the Sub takes the trouble to read it, there will be an indication of what other trades are engaged on the work and what possible difficulties will be encountered in interfacing with them. Make sure that you know that one of the Subs will perform the work described as in the above example - in this case "caulking". (It should be mentioned in the contract format - whatever that is - between you and your Sub).

Give as much time as is required to the preparation of the Scope of Work. It cannot usually be dashed off in a few minutes.

Theoretically, in a construction contract for a large project which has "proper" documentation, the Scope of Work **could** limit itself to a reference to other documents, drawings, specifications, previous work, etc. It **should** be enough simply to say:

"Perform the work in accordance with the drawings, specifications and other documents listed in Section 'X' of the Agreement."

In a few cases, **a very few**, this may be sufficient. The assumption is that the drawings and specifications are totally adequate in every particular - an unlikely proposition. The other danger in being too brief is that **interfaces** *(see Section 2,"Definitions")* may not be adequately covered. As long as there is a starting point and a stopping point, especially where others are involved, there will be **interfaces.** These **must** be clearly defined. Two examples for very small building projects (a renovation and an addition) follow.

You are hanging an exterior door in an existing frame. The Scope of Work reads:

"REPLACE EXTERNAL DOOR

Remove the existing door, complete with hardware, patch existing frame as required to permit proper installation of new hardware. Supply door as per brochure and install same; supply and install all required hardware to manufacturer's instructions. Rub down existing door frame, prime and apply undercoat as required. Paint frame, including interior architrave, to match existing finish. Clean-up and remove debris from site."

The only additional documentation required with this is a brochure showing the type of door, a similar one for the hardware and whatever contract format you are using. For a project of so small a scope, a simple purchase order should be sufficient. Note, in the previous example, that you are not offering to paint the exterior door. Nor are you offering to paint the walls inside the house. Your work stops at the architrave. **This is the point of interface with the existing!** It is not necessary to say that you will **not** paint the door - you have not said that you will. The caution is that you **must** describe the work **completely,** either by drawings, specifications or Scope of Work If there is any part of the description missing that should clearly be there, then the whole scope of work is thrown into doubt and a situation open to dispute is created. You may end up doing some work you had not allowed for.

For instance, were *"and install"* omitted before hardware, there would be a clear question in the mind of the client. A secure installation would require that the hardware be installed: in such a case (that of hardware installation **not** being required) the wording that would make everything clear is to state *"supply only, hardware".*

Simply omitting the word "install" creates a doubt because common-sense and accepted practice also govern a contract. In the example given, of course, you could not *install* the door unless you provided and installed the hinges - part of the hardware. This may seem to be making a mountain of a molehill but, because it seems obvious does not mean it need not be said or written. It might be argued that common-sense requires you to paint the door also. However, because most exterior doors now have a factory finish that is acceptable as is, the Client may not **assume** that you are going to paint it. If you think there might be a misunderstanding you may write *"painting of door by others"*. We are establishing "principles" here, not details

Writing a Scope of Work in sufficient detail makes you *think* in detail of exactly what you are going to do

The General Conditions of the contract or common law based on common-sense and tradition will cover your correcting any damage you might do to other physical elements. Obviously, it is not permissible to knock down the adjacent wall to make it easy to install the door unless you replace it as it was.

A further example: for the installation of a sun-room where there is an existing concrete slab but where another unrelated contractor is providing carpentry and drywall:

"SUN ROOM"

> *The work consists of the supply and installation of a thermally broken, pre-finished, aluminum-framed sun-room with thermopane glazing throughout, all in accordance with the brochure and sketches that form part of this contract. The aluminum framing shall be screw-fixed to a pre-treated wood sill which shall be attached with appropriate masonry screws to the existing concrete floor; flashing shall be as shown on the sketch. The sill only shall be caulked both inside and outside with appropriate compounds. Where end mullions and lintel member adjoin the existing building, the aluminum frame shall be fixed, as appropriate, to existing surfaces or to furring provided by others. Aluminum shall be clean when completed to a condition suitable for caulking by others or to receive cover strips supplied and installed by others."*

What this shows is that others are involved in the total project and that the limits of your work are clear - that you don't do vertical caulking - that there must be a suitable fixing (furring) available - and cover strips are for installation by others; that the client or the other contractor have to know that there are elements **they** have to provide. It also indicates that there is a critical schedule element, because furring has to be provided before you can complete your work. If it is not there when indicated as required in the schedule, then you have a claim for delay.

A Scope of Work may take anything from ten minutes to an hour to write for this sort of job but it can save a lot of argument and, in most cases, a lot of time and money.

The **interfaces** of authority and of task are very important. The coordination element must be clearly shown; in the same way, if there are elements that depend on each other, a reference must be made to indicate precedence of task. This can be shown in the schedule (there **should** be a schedule) and may be referred to in the Scope of Work - though not necessarily so if it is absolutely clear from other documentation. Nevertheless, an additional reference may not be harmful although repetition has its own dangers.

> Many of the techniques described in other sections of this book can assist in the definition of the Scope of Work and interfaces. For instance, depending on the extent to which you detail your Work Breakdown Structure (WBS), you should be able to use it to avoid an overlap of sub-contracts while also ensuring that every task is covered by one contract or another.

Related Work

Another way of drawing attention to interfaces is to mention "related work" (or "associated work", or an equivalent term). While a scope of work for a small project may be simple enough to make clear the requirements of the other players, the more complex the project, the more difficult this becomes. Tying related work into the narrative description (Scope of Work) becomes an exercise in word-play rather than in technical definitions and becomes increasingly difficult the more other contractors or other building elements (not under your contract) are involved.

If you are writing the Scope and find it necessary or easier to include this feature (it is **your** decision), a simple listing under the heading "related work" may be sufficient. You may go further and say "related work by others". In the example given above (the sun-room) you may write:

Related Work by Others: * *Caulking (except sill)*
 * *Rough Carpentry*
 * *Finish Carpentry*
 * *Painting*
 * *Floor Finishes*

No need to mention "concrete" because it exists; rough carpentry is required for your fixings; painting need not affect you but if there are cover strips (finish carpentry), you may assume they will be applied when your work is finished; you know nothing of the floor finishes but, if there are any, they will also follow your work. In a properly documented project, the architect would do all this.

By including "Related Work by Others" you have indicated that you are aware of it, that someone (the Client or the Client's agent or consultant) should make the other trades aware of what you are doing and it is a reminder to yourself to make sure they are all considered in the schedule. The problems associated with a project that has several other separately-contracted trades could substantially affect your price - they **always** cause problems. But you do not **have** to mention "Related Work by Others".

Exclusions

Another way of drawing attention to what you are **not** doing is by listing "Exclusions". (Again, properly done by the "designer".)

"Exclusions" are not quite the same thing as "Related Work by Others" and the use of the term is a bit more risky. Be careful about listing "exclusions" (work to be done by others) though it is often done. What are "exclusions"? Essentially, it refers to work that is not included in your contract but may be thought by some to be so. If you are listing them, do you take the "likely" things that may be mistakenly included in your work? Or do you stretch to the "probable", "improbable" or "highly improbable"? Who defines these terms? Is it possible that any two people would agree on "likely", even though most people may agree on "obvious"?

Scope of Work for Large Contracts

A well-written Scope of Work includes **everything** required for your contract. If you are not sure of what should be in there, where do you draw the line as to what should be excluded? If there are drawings and specs, the problem will not be unmanageable as they are supposed to make these things clear. But, on a large project where there are either other General Contractors or other major trade contractors beside yourself, the problem does arise. If there is a physical overlap or interface where definition is difficult, you may have to exclude what you know is not in your contract but which is sufficiently similar that an error could be made. This Scope should, of course be written by the Architect but the Builder has to realize the importance of looking for it. If there is an obvious problem then the Builder must bring it to the attention of the Architect or Client. If it is permitted to make statements in the tender document, do so by prefixing the description below by writing *"We interpret the contract documents to mean that the work includes all gypsum wallboard work as described ...."*. If the tender documents specifically prohibit commentary, then either make an enquiry before tenders close and ask for an addendum or attach a letter to the bid. Better, far better, to resolve the doubt by an addendum.

A simple example for a large project where trades are split between several contractors is given. Let us take drywall. The properly considered Scope for a drywall contract may say, *"The work includes all gypsum wallboard work as* described in the specifications, both walls and ceilings, between grid-lines "A" and "D" and 1 and 12 but excludes trim for ceiling-mounted air-conditioning registers which are installed across grid-line 12".

The logic is that another drywall contractor will work towards grid-line 12 from grid-line 13 but at a later stage in project implementation. For which reason, the air-conditioning installer will be placing his registers when your work is finished leaving some doubt as to the precise location of the register, for which reason it is better left to the drywall contractor who is **completing** the work.

Logically, the Scope of Work for the other dry-waller will include *"install trim for ceiling-mounted air-conditioning registers that are installed across grid-line 12, being a continuation of this contract of the trim to be installed by this contractor and included in this Scope of Work."* It is the responsibility of the Architect to ensure that this clause is inserted into the Scope of the other drywall contractor. You have done your part in pointing out the interface problem and supplying a resolution. I repeat that doubts as to interfaces such as this one should be resolved before tenders close and should be clarified by an addendum - by the Client or Architect.

Where you are writing the Scope of Work try to avoid the "exclusion" trap; spend the time and effort required to prepare a **complete** Scope of Work. If you do it properly, you need not mention "exclusions". If someone else is writing the Scope (an Architect, for example), check it carefully to make sure it is clear and that you will not risk doing someone else's work or that you include something that does not belong in your contract and so price yourself out of the bidding. No use saying afterward *"I thought that was part of this contract package".*

Acceptable Legal Contract Format

This covers a lot of ground. First "acceptable" to whom? Obviously to the Client and the Contractor but if neither one is sure of the legal implications, "acceptable" is not really good enough.

Then take "legal". An oral contract is "legal" but highly inadvisable - not really "acceptable". A contract of several hundred pages may be "legal" or may not. A contract of two or three pages may be equally or more valid. Because this is dangerous ground more suitable for discussion by lawyers, it is always advisable (if you intend to stay in business) to consult a lawyer, at least to establish the first contract as a standard for your future projects.

The most secure procedure is to use a standard format that has been designed and approved by someone representative of your own and the public's best interests. In Canada, the CCDC formats produced jointly by a variety of professional groups (architects, engineers and contractors) are recommended.

But even when using this standard format, each contract should be seen by your lawyer because the contract format is not the **complete** contract. The complete contract document also includes Supplementary General Conditions, your (or their) Scope of Work, the terms of payment and the drawings and specifications. Any of these could have an error that may get you into trouble. Establish a good relationship with your lawyer; reviewing a simple construction contract is not a big deal - you should be able to arrange a reasonable fee for multiple reviews. But don't expect the lawyer to give advice on the Scope of Work (and certainly not on the drawings and specs.) except in the most general sense - the Builder understands the technical aspects and the lawyer must assume they are correct.

also see Section 4, "Stipulated Price Contract" (pg. 130)

COST OF THE WORK

The Description of the Work (Scope of work), if done in the necessary detail, will give you a sound basis from which to work; the Work Breakdown Structure will provide valuable additional information. Of course, if the project comes with plans and specifications, the problem is simplified; all builders have either studied or learned the reading of plans and specifications. If you haven't, then now is the time to do so. There are plenty of evening courses and many construction associations facilitate this study. It is essential knowledge that you **must** have in order to interpret correctly what the architect or engineer or "design service" is trying to tell you.

But, let it be said now that there are some pretty poor examples of draftsmanship and design going around. If you determine, from the point of view of one who knows his or her subject, that the drawings or specs are inadequate, you are entitled to say so and to ask for clarification or additional details. If, on the other hand, you really want the project and are prepared to bid on inadequate information, be prepared to fight all the way through the construction period.

For the door replacement mentioned in the first example in Scope of Work (above), for estimating purposes you may calculate cost of materials and labour simply as:		Project: Estimate by: Date:		
1	door	$	6 Sub-Total	$
2	hardware	$	7 overhead	$
3	paint	$	8 Sub-Total	$
4	labour	$	9 profit	$
5	disposal	$	TOTAL COST	$

project management for Builders and Contractors

Then again, for anyone with sufficient experience in making claims, inadequate drawings and specs are an invitation to unanticipated profits. But be careful; on the assumption that all contracts could end up in court, make sure you know what may be **assumed** to be in the documents and what has clearly been omitted. If the project is big enough and the potential for gain substantial, there are experts who will help with claims. My advice is to **avoid bidding on inadequate documents**. Issuing inadequate documentation indicates either a lack of expertise on the part of the Client (or the Client's agent - designer) or a willingness to cut corners on the essentials. Not the sort of Client you should prefer; but one you are too often saddled with.

SHOP DRAWINGS

These are not always recognized for what they are. Although usually provided by specialist trade contractors, they may as easily be simple brochures or sketches made on the building site. Either way, they must be considered as contract documents and either they support the design as originally produced or they indicate a modification.

Why should they be considered important in a project management context? Because a great deal of time and money can be saved by considering them during the planning stage and by handling them properly during implementation. The number of shop drawings that you anticipate handling can have a significant effect on your overhead. Reviewing shop drawings is slow and tedious and requires considerable skill. You must either have the capacity to perform the work or ensure that you have someone on staff or available on a contract basis to do it.

Shop drawings will, of course, be reviewed by the designer who must give final approval. But most designers are cunning enough to insert a clause in the contract that makes the Builder or Contractor responsible for their accuracy. There can be a lot of debate about the legality of this but if you find it there, be prepared to minimize the problems by having a review system in place. It is up to the Builder to put a lot of pressure on the Subs providing the shop drawings to make them accurate in the first place.

Any delay in the receipt of shop drawings can delay the whole project - more overhead costs for the Builder and perhaps penalties for delay. Although these penalties can be passed on to the Sub-contractor, if it gets out of hand the Sub may go bankrupt and then everyone loses.

To avoid problems due to shop drawing mismanagement:
- they must be tabulated and scheduled at the earliest possible stage
- required information must be given to the Sub or "Package" contractor in a timely fashion
- the Sub must be reminded frequently of when the drawings are due
- the Builder or Builder's staff must have the technical ability to review them

- they must be reviewed quickly so that they can be returned for changes
- they must be available at the right time for review by the Designer or Client
- on large projects especially, there must be a control system in place
- inspection at the factory or shop may be required of the Builder.

If you receive what you consider a totally inadequate shop drawing, return it immediately with minimal comments. Point out one glaring error and simply note on the drawing "unacceptable". Otherwise you will find yourself doing the suppliers work - and even the Architect's.

"AS-BUILT" DOCUMENTS

Small builders are not likely to encounter "as-builts" but they should know what they are. Simply enough, if the building or structure or installation is changed in any material way, then the original design and/or construction documents no longer reflect the actual construction. So someone has to make sure that all the new information is compiled and recorded.

Large Contractors will be aware of the implications of this. On a major project, it may mean annotating all the drawings and specifications to reflect multiple changes, all at the discretion of the Client and the Designer and over none of which the Builder or Contractor has any control. Make sure there is a limiting clause in the contract that defines exactly what you, the Builder, has to do and either how much time it should take or how much it should cost. A vague clause stating that *the General Contractor shall provide as-built drawings* is not **nearly** enough. Perhaps it is best to ask for a lump sum allowance to defray costs at an hourly rate. This element of management is very difficult to cost. Be sure of one thing; it will cost a lot more than you anticipate!

SAMPLES

Perhaps the only important things to be said about "samples" is a reiteration of the advice given for shop drawings:
- determine what samples will be required during project planning - *this implies a thorough review of the plans and specifications*
- develop a schedule for approvals of samples by the Client - *consider lead times for your Subs to place orders*
- ensure that the Client is aware of the need for selections and has plenty of notice of their date and time
- notify your trades as soon as selections have been made by the Client
- as Project Manager, always attend during selection procedures; do not leave it solely to your Subs
- keep good records and examples of selections - *changes cost money and should be charged to the responsible party (the Client) accordingly.*

CONTRACT DOCUMENT INTERPRETATION

If all contract documents were both correct and clear, builders would be happy to follow their instructions and produce the structure that the Client was expecting to get. Unfortunately, it doesn't work that way; for several reasons. First, the Client tends to change its mind. Second, the design team never has enough time.

The design system is often flawed, anyway, because usually the components of the design are produced in different offices at different rates of production, at different drawing scales. Then there is a tendency to use existing specifications or details that have served well in the past and with "just a minor change" will serve equally well in this case - sometimes with no modification at all. Unfortunately, even with computer-based specifications, making the necessary changes still depends on a human being. And you know how reliable **they** are!

I gave an example in my book *"incredibly easy project management"* of how the problem could be avoided. It involves total control of design and construction being under the authority of one organization. The specific case was a large international contractor having its own total design facilities of which one very important component was the "checkers". This was a group of ex-tradesmen, all of mature years, with donkey's years of site experience. They sat in an office comparing drawings to specifications and drawings to drawings, day in, day out. It was the most soul-destroying job in the organization and the "checkers" were given a lot of latitude in terms of coffee breaks and staring-at-the-wall breaks. But the system worked. They were able to point out inconsistencies to architects, structural, mechanical and civil engineers. Very few errors were found during contract execution - during the actual building stage. Architects, take note; experienced artisans have a lot of useful information.

Most builders do not have the advantage of either such an organization or such a contractual arrangement. But the principle is the same, even if it may only be applied after the fact. A primary task after the signing of the contract is to review all the contract documents against each other for errors and inconsistencies. This is the beginning of the "claim" procedure. A clever contractor can make all his or her profit from establishing early the quantity, nature and cost of all documentation errors or inconsistencies. This has to be handled carefully. It is essential to go all through the scopes of work, specifications, general contract (especially supplementary general conditions) and make sure there are no **valid** catch-all clauses that excuse the differences you find. A Builder needs a nose for these things and must develop a keen sense of what is valid in a contract and what is not. There are no rules for this - it is a matter of experience.

also see Section 3, "Changes and Instructions" (pg. 97)

ESTIMATING

METHODS

There is considerable scope for individuality in estimating methods. Some of the factors which may influence you are the:

- size of the project
- quality and completeness of contract documents - or their total absence
- likelihood of your being awarded the contract - are you really in the running
- time you have available for estimating
- value of work you have in hand
- complexity of the project
- your own estimating skills, and so on

Most common methods are:

1. You consider the job and say "well.....I think that will cost about $xxx", add on a bit for profit and there you are! *You have to be both experienced and lucky for this to work but it is a valid process.*
2. Price per square meter or square foot. This is easier for a new construction rather than addition or renovation and depends on your knowledge of market forces and the amount of experience that you have had with the type of project. *With this one, you have to allow a substantial contingency within your unit of area price to take care of unanticipated requirements.*
3. Estimating by sub-trades. The Builder simply requests prices from Subs, makes sure that everything is covered and adds on a contingency and something for overhead and profit. *Used for both large and small projects, it is safe if you know your Subs and trust both their estimating capacity and their integrity. Your contingency reflects the doubts you may have - more doubts, higher contingency.*
4. The old-fashioned way of taking off a list of materials and labour and pricing it item by item. *This is the most accurate method but has its own dangers. It is a process that is dangerous to interrupt; in other words, you need the time to devote to it without having to break off to put out a fire on another project. Best done by a competent Estimator or Quantity Surveyor (Q.S.) devoted exclusively to estimating.*
5. Using the WBS as a base to arrive at either method 3 or 4. The WBS will split the work into tasks that relate to sub-trades and indicate those things that are not covered and which the Builder or General Contractor will have to take care of. As an aid to a "take-off" by a Q.S. or estimator, it divides the work into manageable elements and can be taken to any level of detail suitable to

project management for Builders and Contractors

the project and the person or persons estimating. It makes it easier for the work to be divided among a large staff. The totals for the tasks or elements are summed later for a total project cost.

The Builder of small projects, renovations and additions is probably his/her own estimator. Which means he/she has to be able to decide on the accuracy of the contract documents or create an adequate substitute if necessary and then have the basic skill to measure up the project. This ability is the foundation of your success; if you can't estimate, you can't be a Builder. When you write the Scope of Work you are in effect preparing a Work Breakdown Structure based on your experience in assembling building elements for a complete project. If you do this well, you will have no trouble preparing a valid estimate. You won't always get the job but you will have the satisfaction of knowing it is for reasons other than poor preparation.

OVERHEAD

Referring to **figure 3 - Organigram**, (pg. 44) it becomes clear also how the Organigram (Organization Chart) can contribute to the estimating that provides the budget for the project. At its simplest, it indicates all the sub-trades that will be required for the project. If there is no additional work by the Builder/General Contractor, nothing more is required (theoretically) than to add up the sub-trade quotations, allow for coordination and supervision by the General Contractor, add building permit, contingency and profit and there you are!
While not believing it is that simple in practice, nevertheless, the principle is. *(You will see that figure 3 as an organigram is very nearly the equivalent of a 2-level WBS. Take just "Builder" and the 7 trades below and you have a WBS.)*

ORGANIGRAM ASSISTS IN PREPARATION OF THE WBS

But that diagram (**figure 3,**) shows something else that must be considered in estimating. There is a Landscape Architect (LA) involved. The LA will be as interested as the Builder in seeing the job completed but it is a fact that, the more designers and/or consultants involved on a project, the more likely are delays. There is an increase in communication requirements, additional paperwork for instructions and changes, more consultation with the Client and so on. All these things take more supervisory time by the Contractor (additional cost) and tend to delay the project (extended overhead, more cost).

This potential for increase in overhead is instantly apparent from the organization chart. If you see an additional consultant, consider the cost; if there are more consultants (Architect, Structural Engineer, Interior Designer, Mechanical Engineer, Landscape Architect, Roofing Consultant, Quantity Surveyor,) they should appear on the chart with their appropriate control and communication lines which will give you a very clear picture of how complex the project may be. It might even frighten you off the project altogether! Such a chart might look like the one that follows:

Figure 7

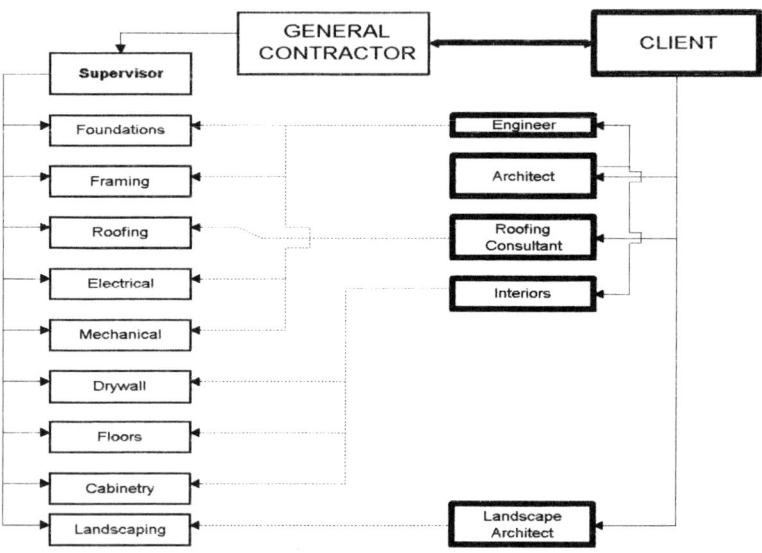

Although it would be irritating to have a project managed in the way shown, this sort of arrangement is not unusual on large projects and illustrates that the Client organization and management can have a serious impact on your project costs. The example above has the Architect controlling the Engineer and the Interior Designer with the Roofing Consultant and Landscape Architect under direct contract to the Client. Once you, the Builder, are aware from the chart, of the complexity of the monitoring (inspection) procedures and the possibilities for independent, uncoordinated activities by the different consultants, you will realize that the possibility of a smooth-running project is seriously jeopardized. Again, more overhead, higher costs.

Reviewing the example, you can see that the sooner you prepare the organization chart the sooner you will realize the project's complexity and the potential for consequent costs. **Figure 4** (pg. 46) and the associated description of the tortuous review procedure makes the point even more strongly. Again, the more bodies involved, the more the overhead increases. Fortunately, this usually does not happen on small projects and there is usually a compensatory increase in potential profit on larger projects. So don't let this deter you completely; just be aware of what may happen.

It is not likely that the Client will submit an Organigram (Organization Chart) when calling tenders but you should be able to infer this information from the contract documents or determine it by questioning the Client or the Architect before tendering. In the case of a small project, simply ask the Client what consultants will be engaged and to whom they will report (who **controls** them). Then make your own chart. For a small project that you know has consultants (say, Architect and Landscape Architect), you may submit your own chart with your proposal and ask for confirmation that you have understood the management (control) system. Ideally, the chart would become a contract document (we shall discuss this later under "Contracts") and any variation after implementation has begun that materially inconveniences you could provide you with a claim for extra overhead or an extension of time.

A frequent situation on small projects is that the Client **may** have an Architect who employs an Engineer and an Interior Designer. On the other hand, the Client **may** employ the Interior Designer by direct contract. This is comforting to the Client but makes life difficult for the Architect. If the Architect has a difficult life, you may be sure that some of the problems will descend to the Builder. More time, more overhead, less profit! The question should be asked (what consultants will be engaged on the project and who controls them?).

> I was engaged on a very large project many years ago where there were inspectors from the Project Managers, Cost-control Consultants, the Design Engineers, the Ministry that was the Client, Quality Control Engineers and Clerks of the Works at every individual building operation. Apart from the occasional brawl between the various inspectors, the job went exceedingly well. but the P.M. was very experienced in handling that sort of overview. It is not for everybody.......... but it proves that it can be done.

CONTINGENCIES

There are two types of contingency to consider; your (the Builder) contingency and the Client's contingency. The first is for you to use as you will and is not disclosed to the Client. The second is included in the project cost under certain circumstances and is directed by the Client.

Builder Contingency

The contingency that you may or may not include in your estimate is based on a number of factors. Theoretically, if you are 100% sure of all the circumstances of the project, then no contingency is required. In fact, there are always unknowns that can only be accommodated by an allowance set aside for those unknowns. Several factors will govern the amount you decide might be required, such as:

- the accuracy of the contract documents

- the expertise you bring to the preparation of the estimate
- the amount of care you are prepared to take with the estimating
- the quantity of unknowns and their magnitude
- the danger of overpricing by reason of casual inclusion of too large allowances

No matter what the number of factors, no matter what weighting you put on the importance of each one, the important thing to remember is that there is no reason why all projects should carry the same contingency percentage. If you plump for 10%, you are obviously aware that it might as well be 9% or 11%. On a large project, one extra percentage point might lose you the contract. Ten percent seems to be a popular figure for a contingency. There is no reason that it should not be 2% or 25% - rationalize the figure; do not just guess at it. Further, you may apply different contingencies to different activities or trades; some are more uncertain than others. You will see this in the Work Breakdown Structure.

> As a consultant monitoring design proposals and production for a Government department, I tried to overturn the concession (or was it a "convention"?) that allowed the designer to generate a contract price 10% over the budget. My theory was and is that if you *allow* a 10% cost overrun, you will always get a 10% cost overrun. Although no-one could dispute my logic, I failed in my endeavour.

So, it is obvious that accuracy in gauging contingency allowances is extremely important. If you have a rotten bunch of contract documents to start with, you are clearly in trouble. The only consolation is that all the other builders who are tendering will have the same problems.

The Builder's contingency percentage varies with each project

First, accept that all projects require different contingency allowances. Consider all the factors that cast doubt on the smooth running of the project; if you use the LFA, look frequently at the "important assumptions"; as they lose their importance during execution of the project or are overcome by clever planning or coordination, so the need for the contingency is lessened. If you want to get into "risk" factors in detail, there are formulae for calculating them - but not in **this** book. Most project managers will be satisfied to be aware of the problem, to take great care in preparing the estimate and to rely on their own experience and expertise to develop the proper contingency allowance. You may modify contingencies as the work proceeds - as you overcome the unknowns, the contingency may reduce. If you can complete the project without using the contingency, then you have that much more profit.

Client Contingency

Tenders or proposals that do not have a strict format established by the Client and that are based on contract documents that are less than complete or non-existent (usually for renovation projects), may be submitted with a contingency allowance for the Client to disburse as required or wished. For example, your proposal may be presented, using the format included in Section 4 "Proposal" (which has a general clause covering the standard of work and materials). An example is given below.

PROPOSAL

A	**FOUNDATIONS**		$ 00,000
1	Excavate and remove spoil from site		
2	Formwork, reinforcement and concrete, stripping & finishing		
B	**FRAMING**		$ 00,000
1	All framing and sheathing to roof level		
2	Windows and exterior doors		
3	Roof trusses and sheathing		
C	**ROOF FINISH**	$ 00,000	
1	Waterproofing and asphalt shingles		
D	**DRYWALL**		$ 0,000
1	Install, tape fill and sand gypsum wall-board throughout		
E	**CABINETS AND DOORS**	$ 0,000	
1	All kitchen and bathroom cabinets		
2	All internal room and closet doors		
F	**PAINTING**		$ 0,000
1	Prime throughout, plus one under-coat and one top-coat latex except bathrooms and kitchen similar coats in oil paint		
G	**ELECTRICAL**	$ 0,000	
1	All electrical roughing-in and finishing		
2	Light fixture allowance ($150.00)		
H	**PLUMBING**		$ 0,000
1	All plumbing roughing-in and finishing		
2	Allowance for special soaker tub ($500.00)		
I	**EXTERNAL WORKS**		$ 0,000
1	Aggregate finished double driveway		
2	2' 6" wide walkway around house; broom finished concrete		
3	Rough grading finish only to garden		
J	**GENERAL**		$ 0,000
1	Clean house and site and remove all debris to environmentally approved disposal		

Sub-Total	$000,000
CONTINGENCY - 8%	$ 00,000
To be disbursed only on instructions of the Client in accordance with receipts and approved time-sheets or by prior agreement with the Builder.	
TOTAL	$000,000

A design/build project creates the greatest problem in respect of contingencies. Often, when the Construction or Project Manager *takes over the project, a certain amount of the design has been completed. This can be checked and a contingency assigned for that part of the construction (it might be in the range of 5-10%). All those parts that are not yet designed - perhaps superstructure or an adjacent building - merit a higher contingency. The most complex sections may have a contingency of 25% or even higher; others that are simpler or more traditional (landscaping perhaps) might only require a standard contingency of 5 - 10%. The point is that **contingency is an enormous variable**. It is never the same even for similar projects nor necessarily the same for elements or units or packages within a project. You ignore this fact at your peril!*

BUDGET - ACCOUNTS

Having developed a budget during the planning of the project (it is part of your Plan of Operation - POP), you must keep careful track of it. Make sure you have a good accounting system that allows you to identify costs against projects (you probably have more than one project running at a time). You must be able to assign each expenditure either to a project (it is easier if they are numbered) or to, say, "equipment", "tools" etc. which then depreciate and become part of your overhead costs. Your bookkeeping must be clear enough that you can assign overhead proportional to your expenditures for each project.

Large Builders will have this system in place but for the small company, it is not a complex matter. If you employ or contract a bookkeeper or accountant, he or she will readily calculate your regular overhead costs as a proportion of your annual business turn-over. You will then be in a position to always say that overhead is a certain percentage of your project estimate - until you become more efficient and can reduce the percentage.

Keep track of all expenditures; do not lose receipts or credit notes; do not leave them on the dash of your pickup until they bake or blow out of the window. You must do your accounting promptly so that you can estimate disbursements at milestones in your project or you will not know until you complete whether or not you are making a profit or losing money?

Save those receipts, invoices and delivery slips!

One Builder I know buys all supplies for one project from one supplier only and for another project, another supplier and so on. This may not be a modern business practice but it works quite well until you run out of suppliers.

If you are using a computer program to track costs it would be an improvement to have one that allows the assignment of costs on the basis not just of projects but of elements, phases, units, tasks or activities of projects. For instance, you may be able to assign your equipment rentals on the basis of a relationship between the tool and the WBS task number or estimate item.

An example: if you are required to rent a pump during excavation because of excess ground water, this could be considered a cost against "Foundations" or if you have taken your WBS to a more detailed level, against "Excavation" as a sub-task of "Foundations". Of course, it is easier to show as disbursed from "Contingency". While that may be technically accurate, it is a bit of a cop-out - if you use "Contingency" indiscriminately, you will find it has become your most important task, just as "miscellaneous" is always the largest file in the office!

It is worth taking the trouble to make your WBS more detailed to permit tracking of costs more accurately. The more accurate your cost control on the current project, the more you will know about the next one. However, **it is a question of degree**. When preparing your estimate, one consideration in deciding how small shall be the tasks into which you break down the project is how effective is your accounting and your ability to track your expenditures. No point in spending hours or days developing 300 tasks and activities if you are unable to monitor and account for them. So when you are making your estimate (your WBS - see below) consider your capacity for tracking your costs during project execution.

But remember that, the more projects you have running concurrently the easier to miss-assign outlays. So, the more important is an adequate accounting system.

WORK BREAKDOWN STRUCTURE

This is as **simple in principle** as the name suggests. It is a breakdown of the **work** into smaller, manageable pieces. But though simple in principle it can become difficult to manage because of its sheer size when expanded and broken down into smaller and smaller units. So the principal skill required in using the Work Breakdown Structure (WBS) lies in deciding the number of levels of detail to suit your estimating, your project organization, your allocation of resources and your ability to track them.

also see Section 3, "Budget/Accounts", above (pg. 72)

The WBS assists in analyzing and classifying the elements (tasks, activities, parts, pieces, units, bits) of a project and may be used for any "project" not just for construction projects. A bicycle, for instance, (considered as a project) may be broken down into major categories. At the first level is the bicycle itself; at the second level are frame, motivating mechanism (pedals and gears), energy transfer (wheels), and guidance system (handle-bars), all of which sum at the second level to the value and quantity of the first level, the bicycle.

In the simplest form of the WBS, these categories are shown at positions, in rows one above the other, on a diagram or chart. By adding a third, lower row on the diagram, you may provide a further breakdown of each of the elements of the second level. For instance, the handle-bars may be subdivided at the third level into stem, handle-bar, handle grips, chrome plating. Each of the other elements at level 2 may be similarly subdivided. The WBS will appear as a pyramid with any number of elements on the bottom row (as many rows as you think necessary and manageable) which, when completed, will eventually produce the top level - in this example, a bicycle.

Against each of these elements, the Manufacturer (or Builder) is now able to assign a cost and a responsible person or group, which information assists in the development of budget, cash-flow, time schedule and assignment of responsibilities.

Simply stated, the WBS does nothing other than describe the project in a manner that makes it easier to understand the individual units and sub-units (tasks) of the project breakdown and to grasp the extent of the project and also to know what is required to complete it. Obviously, to "know what is required to complete it" has degrees of complexity depending on the project. However, approaching it properly through the WBS makes the project **manageable.** What could be more useful than that?

> Many builders prepare their estimates by listing the work by area and then breaking it down into trades, such as:
> Bathroom: wall finishes
>   floor
>   plumbing
>   electrical
>   fixtures
>   accessories
>
> If this list is turned on its side with "bathroom" on the row above walls, floor, plumbing, electrical etc., it will have exactly the same appearance as the WBS charts you will see below. In other words, most **estimates are work breakdown structures** even if they are not thought of that way. *The examples below follow trade breakdowns rather than area.*

A WBS may be introduced at any stage of a project; generally, the sooner the better as it is your best costing and scheduling tool. For those who use the Logical Framework Analysis or Logical Framework Approach (LFA), the WBS may be the next stage in planning. It may even be prepared in parallel with the LFA, though the LFA is the pre-eminent and preferred **planning** tool. *For those who do not like the LFA - it is not **necessary** - just very useful!*

If the WBS is prepared at the same time, it will confirm and add to the information contained in the LFA but may also tend to prolong the exercise. In other words, it may take too much time and be more than you need at that early stage of project development. My preference, **within a large organization**, is to obtain project approval before embarking on a detailed WBS.

A small builder will best arrive at a satisfactory planned end result by means of the Plan of Operation (POP) (with or without the LFA) - and follow with the WBS when **detailed** planning begins and you need a precise estimate to submit to the Client.

> **The WBS for the Small Builder**
> The small builder, not using the LFA, will benefit more from preparing the Work Breakdown Structure as soon as the basic POP is finished as his/her planning period is necessarily much shorter and arriving at an estimate before getting too involved in the project is critically important.

This is one more of those decisions that must be made by the Project Manager (Builder). Some POPs (Plans of Operation) are more detailed than others (a single sheet of paper may be a POP); some contain more unknowns. In large organizations they are often handed to the Project Manager when planning has been completed and approved and implementation or execution about to commence.

In this latter case, starting with the execution or implementation (production) stage, the Work Breakdown Structure may be introduced:

- to assign responsibilities (also see Organigram)
- to explain the project to Team members and to the Client
- to determine what parts, if any, of the project shall be contracted out
- to refine and confirm the cost estimate
- to estimate human resource (personnel) requirements
- to provide a schedule for monitoring units (tasks) of the project and
- to define interfaces

WORK BREAKDOWN STRUCTURE BASICS

To indicate simply how universal are the principles of the WBS, let us take the example of a project to build a bicycle. The *project* may be described as "bicycle" (level 1), the *secondary units* (or tasks) as "structure", "power train", "steering" and "seating" (level 2). This is shown in figure 8 (pg. 76) which has two levels of detail.

figure 8

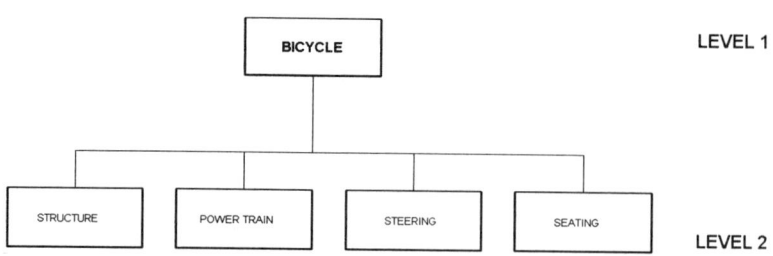

Another example, this time for a construction project - showing only two levels:

figure 9

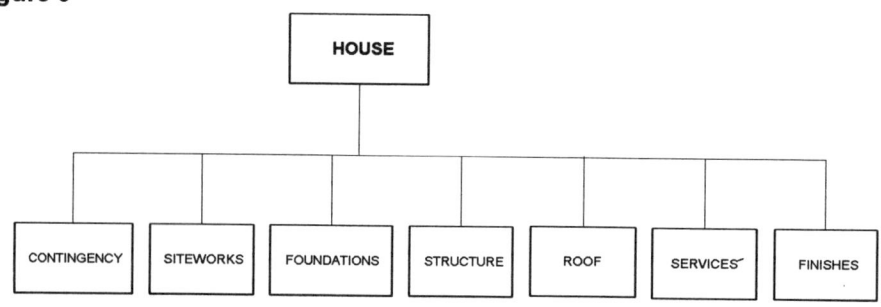

And, similarly, for an overseas aid development project that includes a construction element (the principle is similar for a development project anywhere):

figure 10

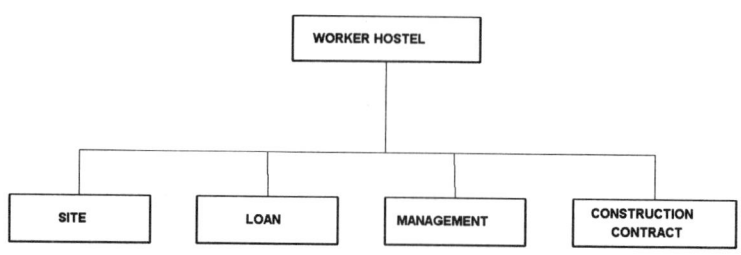

Referring for a moment to the LFA; in the last example (figure 10), "Worker Hostel" is an "output" in the LFA and the second level tasks are "inputs". Note, also, that in that last example (figure 10), each of the

four units at level 2 could (and certainly would) have its own individual WBS. As we are only interested in "construction contract", this unit or task will be considered below.

Each of the three previous examples may be expanded to a third level of detail, to a fourth level and so on indefinitely to the amount of detail that the Project Manager determines will be required to implement the project without creating masses of unnecessary information; and to the capacity of your piece of paper or the memory capacity of your computer.

These lower levels all broaden the available information on "Inputs". Their sum, in terms of cost, across any level cannot be greater than the value of the "Output". Put another way, the sum of the costs at each level is equal to the sum of the costs at every other level and to the final value of the "Output". If I have made that sound complicated, it really isn't. In fact, it may be so obvious as to not need saying. However, I've said it and no regrets!

Let us take the bicycle. If you are simply assembling four units that are purchased from four independent suppliers, then there is no need to break down the second level to a third because you already know all that you need about those units, the design, their cost (from the supplier's quotation) and who provides them (the contracted supplier).

On the other hand, if your factory produces **one** of those second level units, then it is necessary to know what sub-units are required to provide that major unit. So, assuming your factory is providing all the "power train", you may have "gears", "pedals" and "chain" as third level units applying **only** to the power train (all produced in your own factory). See below (figure 11):

figure 11

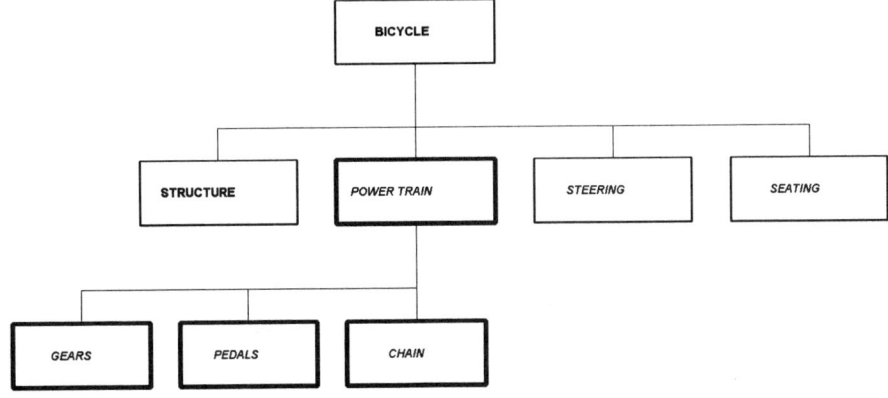

The example for the house (figure 9) may also be expanded to a third level as shown below, where (as an example) one task, "foundations" is broken down into "excavation", "formwork", "reinforcement", "concrete", "strip forms".

figure 12

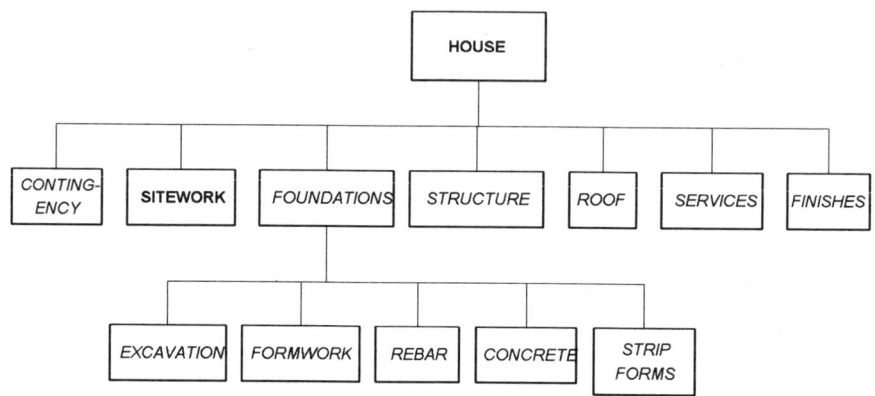

If you are doing this on a piece of paper instead of a computer (and, why not? - paper is still with us), as you develop lower levels of detail for each of the higher units, the whole thing can run off the paper. So start off with a big enough sheet or stick them all together as you go. Get lots of paper and lots of scotch tape.

You need not follow the exact layout shown above. Fit your units on to the page any way that you can, though the "hierarchical" system used so far gives a graphic view of the different levels of value of the units. However, the alternative below sometimes is easier to handle.

figure 13

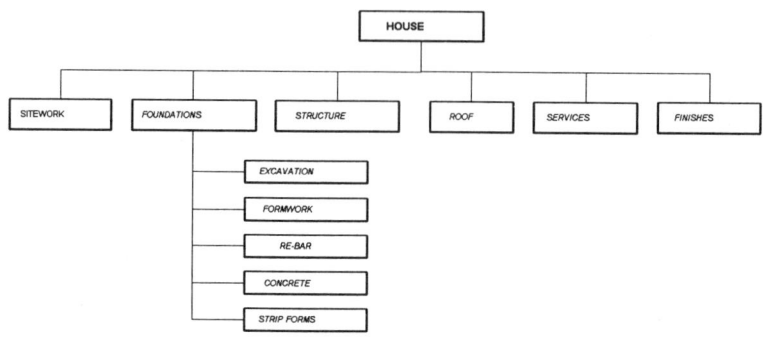

The example for a development project (figure 10 - pg.76) is shown below with "construction contract" broken down into "site-works", "buildings", "inspection", " monitoring (head office inspection and control)" and "maintenance".

figure 14

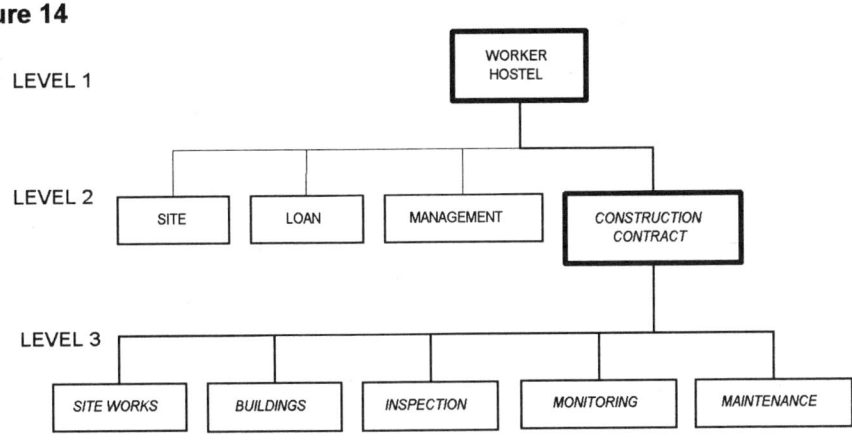

Applying this to a development project in one's own country "Worker Hostel" may be "Golf Club", "Site" becomes "Property Purchase" and the others do not change. The principles of the description that follows are applicable to commercial development projects.

The above WBS is somewhat simplistic as are all the examples. Nevertheless, in the first stages of planning there may be no requirement for more tasks or levels of detail than those shown; they may be expanded later as details of the project become clearer and as money values, responsible parties and other appropriate information is assigned to the tasks (inputs). You may have several different members of staff or consultants working on different units, all to be assembled later.

For this specific overseas aid project and for the benefit of the Development Agency Project Manager (who may know little of construction and who **should** have an expert on his team), rather than for the Builder PM, an explanation follows - but the Builder should also find the analysis useful and should follow it through.

In respect of the construction contract, we are assuming that the project is large enough that it merits being broken down into more economical "contract packages" for contracting purposes. Some reasons may be that local volunteers could clear the site (*Site Works*) of small trees, rocks, fences and so on; in which case, there would likely be no cost involved except, perhaps, the purchase of some hand tools. In such a case, the next level on the WBS would show *Site Works* broken into two tasks, one being *purchase tools* and the other *volunteer labour*. One would have a monetary value, the other (*volunteer labour*) would not.

The buildings may be the subject of one construction contract or several, depending on the nature of the buildings, their size and the capacity of local builders to undertake all or only part of the work.

Inspection is assumed to be an on-site operation to control the quality and cost of the construction. This operation would vary in cost depending (amongst other things) on the sequence of operations. If several builders are employed for reasons of economy or convenience, then the project may take longer because, perhaps, the builders cannot work together on the site at the same time - which may affect inspection costs.

Monitoring (inspection) for this operation is assumed as a head office operation that would vary in intensity during the life of the project, including monitoring during the construction warranty period. That task may be broken down for costing purposes into several smaller activities; these activities would appear on the next lower level of the WBS.

OTHER INFORMATION IN THE WBS

The usefulness of a WBS becomes even more apparent when it is realized that a wealth of additional information can be assigned to each task and/or activity at each level of the chart. The obvious value of the WBS beyond organization of the project - its potential for assisting in estimating and budgeting - becomes clear. Each task or activity (or unit) has a cost or value. This can be assigned on the simpler charts as an elaboration of the box that contains each task, so for Level 3 on the preceding diagram (figure 14):

figure 15

SITEWORKS
$10,950

Further useful information is easily added, for instance, the party responsible for the work, thus:

figure 16

SITEWORKS	
$10,950	General Contractor

And even more information:

project management for Builders and Contractors

figure 17

SITEWORKS	
$10,950	General Contractor
Duration: 28 days	Task No: 1000

The more complex the chart becomes, the more you must resort to a computer to control the WBS. For instance, trying to develop an implementation schedule directly from the duration times shown on a WBS would not be rational if for no other reason than that many tasks run in parallel. A **critical path analysis** becomes essential in such an instance. Critical paths were, at one time, elaborated by hand on huge charts that covered entire walls; not only was this difficult, it tended to be inaccurate as modifications increased and new inter-connections were made. A computer program will do the work now with a degree of security - as long as you feed it the right information! **(Always keep a print-out)** Sometimes you may have to draw out the diagram first in general outline to get a sense of what you are doing.

Breaking down the task shown above (Site-works) into smaller elements or activities, the detail could be made more specific at each additional level. For instance (omitting "durations"):

figure 18

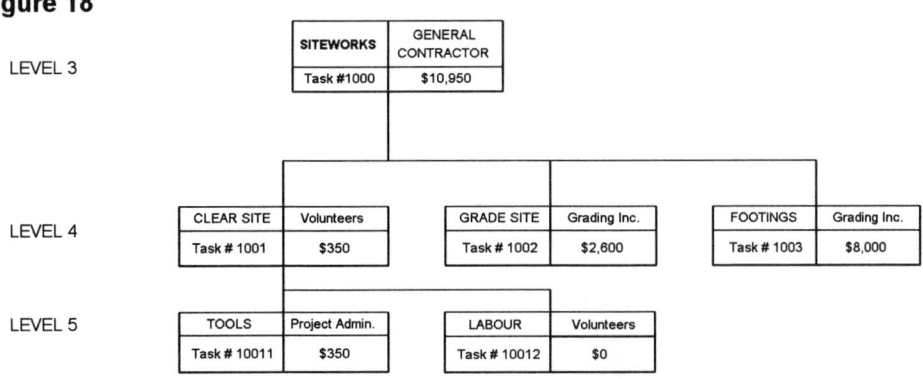

The purpose(s) for which the WBS is to be used governs the amount of information that should be shown or produced. If it is simply to demonstrate work assignment, then there is no need to show cost items and perhaps not even task or activity numbers. If you want to explain how the budget was generated, then clearly costs must be indicated. The important point is to get all the information that will be **really** useful into the computer. And even more important is **not to develop information that no-one will ever use or need.**

Too much information can be more dangerous than too little

Too much information is more dangerous than too little; in the case of too little, there is usually a basis from which to develop more. If there is too much information initially, you may never be able to sort through it and find what you need. This is a very real danger and has happened all too often. Of course, the more complex the chart becomes, the more important becomes the computer and the ability to use it properly.

Another point; if your detail expands to near the maximum capacity of your computer, you either have a program that runs so slowly as to be an agony or you run the risk of over-loading and crashing the program. It is disastrous to lose all those hours of work simply because you try to cram too much into your computer.

Do not put more information into your Work Breakdown Structure than you need or than the computer can handle

SUMMARY OF THE WBS

The "art" of the Work Breakdown Structure (WBS) is to decide the level of detail that is required for the project. It varies with a number of factors such as the size of the project, the type of sub-contracting, the number of sub-trades involved (in the case of construction) and so on. In the examples given so far, a maximum of three horizontal levels of the WBS are shown.

Referring to the example in **figure 9**, there are 7 tasks or units at level 2, of which one is "Contingency", plus 6 major "packages" for the house. Theoretically, it is possible to sub-contract the whole project by writing 6 contracts for these "packages". In such a case it would be very important to ensure that **everything** were covered. The only task for the General Contractor would be supervision and administration. That could be shown as the sixth package at that level but, during these preliminaries, it is assumed to exist within the first level. "Contingency" is shown as a separate item because it may be substantial in both scope and cost, depending on what is likely to have been missed in the contract "packages" (it could also be applied at the next lower level to each task).

Stage 2 of this WBS, shown in **figure 12** indicates "Foundations" broken down into 5 smaller units (or "tasks") at the next level of detail. Potentially, each of these 5 items could be broken down further. "Sitework" may show at the next lower level as "Clear Site", "Mass Excavation" and "Blasting". So at this third level, we might assume the possibility of at least 3 activities for each of the 6 above which would be 18 for that level.

Extrapolate this and one could **guess** at 18 times 6 activities at the next and final level - a total of 108 activities. In reality it depends on how the project is estimated, how it is contracted and how it is monitored. No point in listing 108 items if there is insufficient time and personnel available to make sure they are performed and performed properly once the project starts on site. (Note that as you reach lower levels of the WBS, each subsequent breakdown will be more and more detailed).

As it happens, **figure 12** shows 5 activities for "Foundations" at level 3; using **that** as a guide for all the tasks at level 2 would give a total of 300 activities at level 3. You can see how soon this gets out of hand!

> The WBS is your main estimating tool. The more detailed, the more accurate but also the more difficult to handle. You really cannot avoid using a computer if you need to make repeated calculations of an estimate. A simple spreadsheet program will usually be sufficient.

"Site-works" is enlarged in the example (**figure 18**) to show the information usually attributed to each package of a WBS, namely "responsible party" and "cost". If every item is costed at this level, then the total cost of the project can be readily calculated. The amount of detail shown is not usually required in residential construction but becomes useful in multi-task projects (a multiple housing project) where the tasks are not identical or where there are variations, for instance, in depth and type of excavation, giving different costs for some elements of each house.

When a project may potentially be split into a number of "packages", the WBS may be considered in a slightly different way. The essential requirement is to relate it to your contracting methodology.

As an example, let us suppose that the overseas development project previously described **(figures 10 & 14)** is a substantial construction project of several buildings, a "Worker Hostel" comprising 4 large distinct buildings and a community centre. In **figure 14**, this element of the total project is shown at level 2 as "Construction Contract". It is broken down into 5 tasks at level 3 (the next lower level) - "Site-works", "Buildings", "Inspection", "Monitoring", and "Maintenance". *(If this is beginning to worry you - don't let it. It is really simple logic and I hope I have not made it complicated!)*

This "Construction Contract" is, in effect, a sub-WBS of the overall development project. In a typical project management "Team", different team members would be responsible for the units at level 2 - a financial expert to organize the "loan", the Project Manager would take care of the "management" element and the Field Supervisor would probably manage the "site" task which was to comprise both volunteer labour and purchase of some hand tools. **This is of no consequence to the "Builder" (building Project Manager) who is estimating and organizing only the "Construction Contract".**

Figure 19, on the next page, takes "BUILDINGS" from level 3 of figure 14 and starts it in this sub-WBS as being at level 1. It is first broken down into major units (sub-projects) of 5 separate buildings. Each of these will again have its own WBS; the example shows "Building 1" as being split at level 3 into 6 major tasks.

Now the expert must decide. Is it to be tendered as 6 sub-contracts or is it, perhaps, to be handled by Construction Management (CM) techniques? - in which case a detailed further breakdown would be required to a considerable number of additional levels. If it is to be tendered as 6 sub-contracts, the WBS can stop at that level (3). There is a temptation to do just that - the easy way!

figure 19

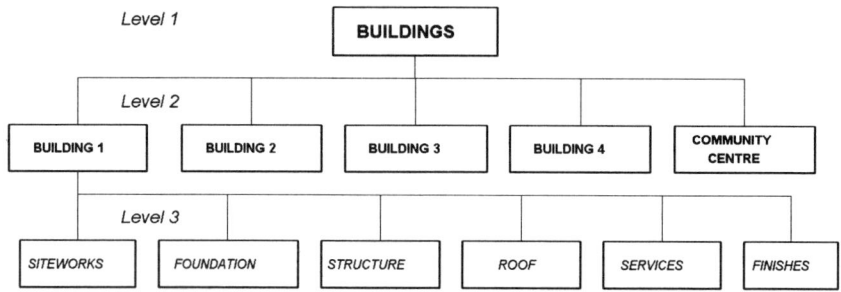

Would this project be even easier to manage if broken down into 5 separate "contract packages" at level 2? The answer depends on practical administration problems, contracting methodology and site control conditions.

This is where the intuition and experience of the Project Manager (or his/her advisor - if the PM is non-technical) is important. It is impossible for this book to indicate solutions because the answers vary for every project and every organization implementing the project. However, some of the complications that may occur are described below.

Administration

If you have a computer with a lot of memory, the amount of detail (the number of tasks and activities) should not be an impediment to handling the project as a whole (that is, the 5 buildings or "contract packages" in one WBS).

If you are restricted to pencil and paper, it would be easier to arrive at a budget by splitting the project into "packages"; then simply add the totals. It would also be easier this way to schedule the work when construction starts. You would need 5 schedules with 5 start dates following each other.

On the other hand, if you want all the work to proceed at the same time (concurrent packages) dividing it into 5 "packages" **with individual WBSs** makes it more difficult to assign human resources (personnel) because it limits your view of the whole project at any one time. It does not provide a complete "overview" of the project. It also requires a clever cross-checking and scheduling system for the procurement of materials in order to take advantage of bulk buying for the total project. Of course, a good computer program will do these things for you.

Contracting

It might be convenient to contract the 5 packages to 5 general contractors. This has the disadvantage of probably increasing **total** cost by reason of 5 overhead organizations and profit mark-ups. It also could create site control problems because of shortage of physical space on the site as each contractor would need an office and storage space (for equipment, access, materials etc.). On the other hand, properly controlled, all working at the same time, it should expedite completion of the work.

If the entire project were managed by one General Contractor (GC), there would be a theoretical saving on overhead and even on profit. It would be less costly, too, in sub-contracting terms because the GC could have trade sub-contractors moving sequentially from building to building. But this might extend the schedule of construction by not having the advantage of work proceeding on all buildings at the same pace at the same time.

Site Control

Inspection costs are likely to increase if contracting is by 5 general contracts. Assuming that construction progress is roughly in parallel for each "package", then all trades would be working on 4 similar buildings at the same time (the community centre would most likely be different in respect of trade percentages of cost). This could mean that inspection requirements are more demanding, in fact that another half-inspector is required. As half-inspectors are not generally available, it means either doing without, taking on a whole inspector and spending more money thereby or finding a competent part-time worker.

This is bad enough from the point of view of the builder, developer or general contractor but also becomes a problem for the Project Manager running an overseas or even a home-based development. Remoteness from the site is naturally worrying. There are not always competent supervisors or inspectors available locally. Does this mean more inspection from head office, more overseas or other long-distance travel costs and so on? All of these considerations apply to one degree or another to development projects in your own country; a project in the next state, province or county can be difficult to monitor and more costly in terms of overheads.

THE WBS AND THE COMPUTER

The answer to all these questions is to prepare a **series** of WBSs that examine the variations in management technique and contracting practice. If the project is anything more than minimal, this becomes hell without a computer program. So, if you are considering any project that suggests the possibility of requiring to be split into packages, make sure you have a good computer program available - most of them have "what-if" scenarios. But, don't forget that the computer is your tool. Only **you** can give it useful data and useful variables. The availability of a suitable computer program and a competent operator could be a critical factor in deciding whether or not to split the project based only on the assignment of personnel. Ultimately a decision is required. This is the hard part: all the data in the world cannot replace the experience that makes that decision possible. An experienced and intuitive Project Manager is worth his/her weight in lap-top computers.

The above example serves equally for a Project Manager working for a Builder or Contractor as for a Project Manager of a property developer or development agency (NGO). For that matter, a manufacturer would encounter the same problems in a slightly different context.

I apologize for hedging all this around with "should", "could", "may", "potentially", "perhaps", "on the other hand" and so on. But the point is that it is important to **be aware of the problems**, how each variation in one management element "may" create a problem in another.

A saving in contract costs might mean an increase in inspection. You might think that an increase in inspection cost is not likely to be a major item and you may be right. But it has often happened that the anticipated increase is so small that management ignores it as a requirement or, perhaps, a suitable person might not be available (reliable inspectors are very hard to find) and, consequently, not being properly considered and not having an adequate budget, the work is badly performed resulting in either delays for remedial work or additional charges, some of which rub off, one way or another, on to the Client and an **unanticipated** cost is generated. So a higher **project** cost is generated due to short-sightedness in a simple matter of inspection. This is a frequent management error. Do not let it happen to you.

Budget and Resources

Computer programs eliminate or at least minimize possible budget problems that occur in traditional paper-generated budgets when projects are split into packages. The problems with paper are mainly logistical; the possibility of error increases as figures are transposed from packages and assembled into totals related to the authorized budget. With care, there should be no problem but a computer does it more reliably. I repeat, this is not guidance towards a solution but a statement of some of the factors to be considered. To summarize some important points. In considering whether to divide a project into "packages" (sub-projects) examine:

- the Project Manager's capacity to manage the project as a sole project
- feasibility of several GCs operating on the site at the same time
- inspection personnel availability
- possible cost increases due to multiple contracts

- possible cost increases in remedial work due to lack of inspection
- head office monitoring costs - *often assumed to be part of "overhead"*

and also:
- insurance problems due to conflict between packages (this is a subject in itself beyond the scope of this book but keep it in mind).

APPROVALS

All Builders have to face the possibility of delays caused by "approvals" at various levels and by various organizations. Both large and small Builders and developers need approvals in respect of:

- planning permission
- building permits
- inspections of Authorities having jurisdiction over the work
- material and equipment samples
- shop drawings
- interim payment certificates
- Site Instructions and Change Orders
- as-built drawings and specs
- final approval of the Architect or the Client - *if it is a design/build project, the approvals are even more demanding*

And within a large building organization there are internal approvals at different levels of authority through all the planning and construction phases (Boards of Directors, Supervisors, Committees).

My book ***"incredibly easy project management"*** devotes a few pages to this subject as it is found in a bureaucratic or commercial environment. For now consider that, if you know there are going to be "approvals" required, then you must plan for them. Make sure that those doing the approving are aware of the requirement and when it or they will be required. Weigh small points such as the intrusion of a week-end into the approval process (don't ask for an approval on Friday afternoon!). If Board of Director approval is required make sure you have documents ready for their regular meeting. Do not be satisfied with advising an "approver" just once; make sure he, she or they is/are constantly aware that the requirement is approaching and that failure to decide will jeopardize the project. Be persistent.

For the small builder especially, the most difficult "approval" to obtain is often that of the Client for finishing materials or fixtures. The Client tends to procrastinate or change its mind. What type of tiles for the bathroom, the pattern for the vinyl floor-covering, the paint colour in the living room, all the dozens of things for which there are a hundred alternatives. Make sure that the Client knows of these approvals ahead of time and make sure you get them as you need them. This is your responsibility, not the Client's. If the Client misses appointments that have been clearly and adequately notified and confirmed, write claiming an additional cost of supervision, transport, etc. plus overhead and lost profit.

> *In respect of notifications, should you not receive a response to a proper notification to any party (Client, Consultant, Contractor), write, with sufficient lead-time, saying that you will proceed as outlined unless notified in writing to the contrary. Always make sure that the notification has been received - courier or mail receipt.*

COORDINATION AND INTERFACES

SITE COORDINATION MEETING

Bringing your sub-contractors together in a productive working relationship is not always easy. Often they do not know each other; if they do, they may be unsympathetic toward each other. Perhaps your contracts with them will not be a significant part of their work load. For which reasons it is important to plan a site meeting well in advance to introduce the schedule, to develop the interfaces and to establish your supervisory techniques. This is a good time to introduce the organigram if it has not already been done, especially if there are consultants involved in the project.

I do not suggest you try this for a small improvement (renovation/addition) project but anything substantial that involves several trades and any unusual aspects, such as the unknowns in **large** renovations or additions, deserve discussion between those involved. It is standard practice on large projects. Do not neglect it on smaller ones that are anything other than absolutely straightforward.

INTERFACES FOR ADDITIONS AND RENOVATIONS

The interfaces on a standard house construction are generally well known. Your Subs will relate to the schedule in a standard and generally acceptable manner. Renovations and additions are not the same. The connections between existing services and new have to be carefully considered both to avoid inconveniencing the Client and to ensure that the different trades work in a proper sequence. Try to show these interfaces in your schedule; bring them to the attention of the Subs at the first coordination meeting; write a memo if that is the only way you can get the information out. Do not rely on a 'phone call or a message on an answering machine. Anything significant in respect of coordination must be **written** somewhere - and must be known to be communicated. Check to make sure the information arrived and is understood.

It must be written! It must be *known* to be communicated

LABOUR-ONLY CONTRACTS

If the Builder is providing materials to a "labour-only" Sub-contractor, ensure that materials arrive on time. The schedule will have been discussed; the delivery of materials should be planned to meet the needs of the Sub. If the Sub is there and the materials are not, there could be a charge to the Builder for lost time.

INSPECTIONS AND APPROVALS

"Approvals" have been mentioned above. Make sure that Sub-contractors are aware that they are known and scheduled. As often as not, it will be the Sub that determines technical inspections (electrical and plumbing) - within the Project Manager's schedule. The Builder/Project Manager will make sure they fit the schedule and that everyone is aware of them.

CONTRACT ADMINISTRATION DOCUMENTS

The first site meeting is a good opportunity to demonstrate Site instructions and Change Orders. There is nothing unduly complex about either one but familiarity will make them more acceptable. If you intend to retain proper control of the project, they are essential and your Subs must be aware of their existence and their nature as early as possible." More paper", you complain but you **must** do these things.

also see Section 4 "Documents" (pg. 129)

SUPERVISION

PLANNING

Take account of Supervision in your Plan of Operation. Make its impact clear in your Sub-contracts or Purchase Orders - make sure it is **obvious** - that the Subs know that proper supervision is important to you as a Builder, that it is going to happen, that you will be on the site to assist all concerned in integrating the different trades and will make sure that everything is done properly. The best occasion to convey this emphasis is at the site coordination meeting of your Sub-contractors.

If the project is very small and a site meeting not reasonable, you may convey the message in your final negotiation with the Sub by saying something inoffensive but obvious such as *"I shall be spending a lot of time on the project and shall give you whatever assistance I can to make your job easier. I shall be keeping a close eye on the other work to make sure that you are not hindered in any way."* The message is that you will spend a lot of time on the site and will be keeping an eye on **everybody.** The Purchase Order in Section 4 leaves no doubt that the Sub-contractor must perform properly and that he/she may lose the contract should performance be less than expected. The General Conditions of the Builder's contract with the Client are equally forthright and, as they should be reviewed by the Subs, make the fact of compliance even clearer.

The Supervisor (or Project Manager as Supervisor) is responsible for many less-than-obvious things that, if you develop a job description for the Supervisor, may be described in an introductory phrase such as *"...... ensure compliance with the contract documents in the execution of the work and take all steps necessary to create and maintain a proper environment for the integration of elements of the construction into the Work"*.

This broad phrase and what it implies should be **understood** as necessary by the small builder/contractor and should be **established** by the large contractor as a part of the job description contained in a Procedures Manual. For a large project with several or many supervisory staff (and particularly on a Construction Management project) the Job Description should be prepared to include, as a minimum, the following:

- Report to - *the person immediately superior - only* **one** *person*
- Responsibility - *a broad description of the Supervisor's "accountability" - this is* **not** *a list of* **activities**
- Activities - *the actions required of the Supervisor; the operations to be performed*
- Report Procedures - *oral and written reporting requirements - to whom, about what and how often*

"ATTITUDE" AND SUPERVISION

This is where "attitude" is important. The Supervisor should **want** to ensure not only that the work meets the standards of the contract documents but also that the work site is safe, that it is clean (to the extent possible), that it does not inconvenience adjacent properties or public access, that necessary insurance is in place, that the workers have all their legally-mandated facilities, etc. Supervision is not simply an exercise in over-viewing activities; it is also an active pursuit of preparatory activities that permit the Work to proceed as it should. For which reason it must be thought about during the planning phase.

Supervision is also a preparatory activity

PROJECT DIARY

If the project is large enough it should have its own diary ("large enough" by my definition means when you have at least one supervisory person on-site for about 66% of his/her time). Smaller projects will join their companions in your current diary (**of course**, you have a diary, don't you?). Note down all the critical dates before the project starts; milestone achievement dates, major deliveries, meetings, early and late dates for Client selection of materials, etc. Activities or tasks that you consider critical to the success of the project should be flagged a few days or a week ahead of time by another diary entry such as *"Cabinet installation next Tuesday, July 18"*. There will be an entry on the date itself.

Flag essential decisions in your diary

It is incredible how few small builders and contractors take the trouble to forewarn themselves in this way. How long does it take to make such an entry? - just a few seconds. It can save you big headaches. It can also warn you if the project is slipping behind schedule. If you do nothing else that this manual recommends, at least keep a business diary and/or a project diary!

CONTRACTS

An orderly mind in a Builder allows him/her to see things in their legal context. Any financial relationship between two parties is governed by the terms of an agreement or by common law (traditional precedents). So if a builder/contractor asks someone to do something for which payment is or will be given, a contract exists in a legal sense - an "oral" contract.

If a problem occurs, as a last resort one party may sue the other and the courts will resolve the dispute based on the law of the country or district that has jurisdiction over the work and what is "reasonably" understood to be the agreement. You don't want the problems associated with disputes, so **oral contracts are a bad idea**. Always make sure that the agreement is **written**.

No matter how careful either party is, there is always the possibility of disagreement. The most complex and detailed written contracts are open to some degree of interpretation. However, common-sense demands that you try to minimize the problems. Common-sense also decrees that you have to be rational in developing contracts; there is no point in paying a lawyer $100 to produce an agreement for work valued at $300. So let common-sense prevail. But do not persuade yourself that no written contract is necessary. Some sort of **formal agreement is required for every business relationship** no matter how small the transaction.

For the Builder, this means that there must be a formal agreement with the:
- Client
- Sub-Contractors
- Suppliers
- Employees

All business relationships require a formal, written agreement

CLIENT

The major problem with a Client/Builder contract is deciding how much detail is required. Clients contemplating small projects are often made nervous by a lengthy document even though it is as much or more to their advantage as to that of the Builder. Most professional organizations of architects, engineers and contractors' associations in different countries, states and provinces have standard documents that can be adapted to most requirements.

I recommend that even the smallest project have such a contract, no matter how unwieldy it may seem. If you want to make it less frightening, have the General Conditions (usually the most extensive part of the contract) printed in very small type on both sides of the paper so that, at least, it is not bulky. An adaptation of some of these contract formats is included in Section 4 in this book and is also available from the Publisher on a computer disk (WP6.0a). *(I have used translations of this particular contract format in both Costa Rica and Portugal. The only major adaptation being references to their overriding national codes.)*

This is your most important contract and there are certain essential elements that all such contracts, long or short, **must** contain. They are:

- Agreement - *this is the part that is signed and tells what the contract comprises - documents etc.- and what is its value*
- Scope of Work or Description of the Work
- Contract Price - *in the Agreement*
- Terms of Payment
- General Conditions
- Supplementary General Conditions - *sometimes*

If there are drawings and specifications, they will also form part of the contract and will be listed in the Agreement. They should also be initialled by both the Client and the Builder who will each have one original copy of the full contract documents. Other copies of the drawings and specs are provided to the Builder for use in the actual construction - customarily about 5 sets. For medium and large projects, I also prefer to attach an Organigram if there is no indication of the organizational structure by the Client or the Architect.

If you are not accustomed to stipulating all these things in a contract, do not be dismayed by them. There is really very little to it. Be reassured that:

- the General Conditions might give you trouble if you had to write them from scratch but someone else has already done that for you
- you know what the Scope of Work is because you have made an estimate
- there is no problem with the cost of the work (again, because you have made an estimate) and ....
- you know that you want payments as the work proceeds
- supplementary General Conditions are a rarity in small projects and pretty obvious in their implications

What you do have to take care with is how you present the information; a little extra trouble at the beginning - getting your documents in order and neatly typed is important. There will be examples in Section 4 of this book.

One more important point for the small Builder. The contract format provided in Section 4 may seem more than you need. The Proposal format in the same section may seem insufficient. You may decide that something in between would be suitable. I advise you not to try to achieve that by eliminating clauses of the General Conditions that you may decide are not applicable. The long contract covers all your needs; the proposal format is acceptable because it does not pretend to be something it is not. Mess with the long format and you are almost guaranteed to lose an important clause. There is such a thing as Murphy's Law!

SUB-CONTRACTORS

Probably the easiest way to handle a sub-contractor agreement is to issue a Purchase Order that describes the work and add something such as:

"This contractor agrees to perform the work described in accordance with the regulations, codes and standards of good workmanship governing and appropriate to this trade. This contractor understands and accepts that the terms and conditions of the contract governing the agreement between the Client (Owner) and the General Contractor, shall apply equally to the terms of this Agreement".

The Purchase Order included in Section 4, "Documents" covers this in a more general but equally demanding form.

The contract between the Client or Owner and the General Contractor will contain clauses that make clear the relationship of the Client to the Sub-contractors - **there is none** - but that is spelled out in the General Conditions of the contract. The Subs should already be aware of this (unless they are complete amateurs) or be made aware by supplying them with a copy of the General Conditions. This really is not a big deal. Most small trade contractors on small projects will consider the whole procedure a little hysterical, will probably not bother to read the General Conditions but, you, the Builder, will have covered yourself by supplying the information.

Often, a Sub-contractor will make a proposal or give you an estimate in a format that simply requires your acceptance by a signature. This is acceptable but you should go further and note on your acceptance that the General Conditions and the Schedule also form part of the Agreement with the Sub. If the Sub has not seen them, attach them to your acceptance. It is still better to use your own Purchase Order, perhaps attaching the Sub's estimate to that document.

SUPPLIERS

Most material suppliers already have established terms for the purchase of goods and supplies. Often they are outlined on the back of either a delivery slip or an invoice. As a matter of policy, you should make a point of asking your major suppliers if they have any special terms such as acceptance of material returns and re-stocking charges. If you don't like the terms, there is not a lot you can do about it other than change suppliers.

EMPLOYEES

This last one is easy enough as it is covered by the labour laws of every modern state. If you don't know them and/or are not abiding by them, you are already in deep trouble. If you thought that you did not have a contract with your employees, you had better talk to a lawyer or an accountant.

SUMMARY

To summarize the main points. A Client/General Contractor contract should have:
- **acceptable legal contract format**
- **description of the work**
- **price for the work**
- **time (execution) schedule** - *this is sometimes simply dates to commence and finish but a detailed schedule is preferable for both parties*

- **organigram** (organization chart) - *not a legal requirement but strongly recommended*

A Sub-contractor contract should have:
- **purchase order**
- **description of the work**
- **price for the work**
- **time schedule**
- **copy and acknowledgement of the General Conditions of the main contract**

CONTRACT TYPES

A contract can be whatever the parties agree that it shall be. Nevertheless, it always falls within the legal context of the Government of the country, state, province or whatever sovereign body applies the law. In respect of payment, there is also considerable variety. Some of the more common forms are:

- Stipulated price - *sometimes called lump-sum*
- Cost Plus
- Time and Material plus Overhead plus Profit
- Time and Material plus Fee
- Construction Management Fee (see below)

STIPULATED PRICE
Perhaps the most common format and the most popular with the Client because it is the most clearly defined with all the conditions, total cost, duration, etc. known before the work commences. The disadvantage to the Builder is that he or she generally builds an essential cushion (contingency) into the price to take care of errors and omissions and, in a competitive bid, this may push the price too high. The amount of the cushion is a product of:

- the quality of the contract documents
- the certainty of the Builder of his/her estimate
- whether the Builder has been able to obtain firm estimates from the Subs.
- how badly you, the Builder, want the work
- and a few other things

Stipulated price is particularly difficult for the small builder who is working without adequate contract documents on an addition or a renovation. In such a case, one way to escape the danger of under-bidding is to include "Lump Sum Allowances" (or Prime Cost Sums) for items of which you are in doubt.

In the Proposal you might write, for instance:

"All electrical work to applicable codes and the requirements of authorities having jurisdiction (Lump Sum Allowance $860.00).

The $860 is included in the total price as are any other Lump Sum Allowances (LSA). Should the work for that particular item cost less, the difference is returned to the Client. Should it cost more, the Client is expected either to pay the extra or reduce the contract specification to meet the amount of the LSA. The Client must be notified well in advance if the LSA is found to be insufficient - he/she must be given the option of cutting down on something.

COST PLUS

The least desirable type of contract, in my opinion. The Client may find it acceptable at first but usually the charm fades as the cost rises. A large Builder may find it acceptable because overhead is a relatively smaller percentage of cost than it is for the small Builder. A Builder/Contractor of substantial reputation who can be relied upon to perform the work according to the prevailing acceptable standards is in a position to establish a "chargeout" rate for his workers that will take care of all overhead and incidental costs with a margin included for unforseen costs. Add 10% profit and that is a good deal. However, for most of the industry, the base rates to which percentages are to be added is liable to be the subject of a lot of discussion with the Client.

If the small Builder is prepared to accept a mark-up of, say, 15% plus 10% he or she may get the contract but lose money. A rational charge should be about 25% for overhead and 10% for profit. Even at this, the amount of supervisory time devoted to cost plus work is so high as to make the profit doubtful. An alternative is to include a charge for supervisory time which would be "cost plus supervision plus profit". The Client is more likely to accept this than the 25% plus 10%. I have done cost-plus work as a Builder and hated it. I have supervised cost plus for a very large Contractor that made a mint at it!

Obviously, there are no norms that apply to every project, every Builder and every Client. This is simply a warning to look carefully into the implications of "cost-plus". Make sure that the Client understands the meaning of the term and make it clear what he/she is paying for and if there is an "upset" limit on cost. For yourself, be sure that you understand the financial implications of what you are offering. Cost-plus is not necessarily or even usually a quick route to a large profit. It sounds good and, properly planned and considered, may be a good deal. Before you sign the contract, make sure you may reasonably anticipate a profit.

TIME AND MATERIAL - Plus Overhead Plus Profit

A method that is fair to both parties but time-consuming in administration. All time-sheets have to be authorized by the Client or the Architect. All materials must be checked onto the site or be seen to be included in the work; an agreed overhead and a profit as a percentage of the cost is added to the Time and Material. The method precludes the use of Sub-contractors on the basis of a lump sum bid to the General Contractor - they must provide time-sheets also. All very cumbersome but rational. Not often used for a variety of reasons - one of which is the obligation of the Client or his/her Agent to verify all time-sheets and material deliveries and the essential requirement of ensuring that the materials and labour are really contributing to **this** project and not some other.

TIME AND MATERIAL PLUS FEE

Similar to the preceding method but a fixed fee is agreed for the supervisory, overhead and profit elements of the contract. An "upset" final cost of time and material is usually stipulated in the contract - a sum that will not be exceeded without authorization of the Client. It is still necessary to monitor time-sheets and materials but the Client knows the amount of the overhead and profit in advance - unless the upset figure is exceeded by authority of the Client. In which case the fee should be increased. Again, a great deal of inspection is required by the Client or the Agent.

also see Construction Management, "Fee Structure" (pg. 102)

CHANGES AND INSTRUCTIONS

A contract may be modified or extended by an instruction from the Client or the Client's Agent. This should never be just by word of mouth. It **must** be written. This applies to all contracts and contract changes, large or small, to all Builders and Contractors large and small.

More trouble and bad feeling is caused by the acceptance of an oral instruction than by most other interchanges between Client and Builder. Often it is either too much trouble or too difficult to describe or there is insufficient time or there is no proper format or no system in place or a dozen other reasons that make writing an instruction an inconvenience.

If it is too difficult to describe, then there is little chance of the required change being interpreted to meet the approval of the Client. This is one of the things that all Builders must learn to do well. In fact, it is more important to the Builder doing an addition or renovation than is the case with a large project where the cost of an error may be absorbed. A change that goes wrong can end up being a substantial percentage of a small contract's value.

SITE INSTRUCTION

In Section 4 of this manual is a Site Instruction format. Have some printed or photocopied and keep a supply of them handy. If the Client wants something that is not in the original contract, write it out in sufficient detail to eliminate doubt as to what is being requested and provided. You don't want to hear "That isn't what I wanted" after the work is done. If it is possible to calculate the price immediately, include it; if you know it will extend the contract time, say so. You are not **required** to be specific about schedule extension because the Site Instruction will be followed by a Change Order when you have the time to do it.

If it is not possible to quote a price immediately, you may write "Subject to confirmation by Change Order". Get the Client to sign the Site Instruction. I cannot emphasize too strongly that any interchange between Client and Builder that involves a change to the Contract must be in **writing.**

Then prepare a Change Order as soon as possible and submit it with the price breakdown and any extension of schedule. You may find that the Client has changed his or her mind after seeing the price but, at least, you will both know where you stand.

All contract changes must be authorized in writing

CHANGE ORDER

A Change Order is a customary method of modifying a contract by agreement between the Client and the Builder/Contractor. It describes the change and justifies the cost (it could be a credit, an extra or no change in price) and the extension or reduction of time, if there is any. It also shows the original contract price and the cost of all the Changes, added up to justify the revised contract price. There is a format in Section 4, "Documents". Although this is the official and proper way of keeping a running check on both the work and the cost of the work, the Site Instruction, if priced by the Contractor and signed by both parties, is also a contract document and sufficient of itself to validate the extra cost; but it should be followed by a Change Order to up-date and confirm the revised total cost of the work.

CHANGE ORDERS IN CONSTRUCTION MANAGEMENT

The noteworthy thing about Change Orders under Construction Management (CM) is that there are usually a lot more of them. By the nature of the contract there is more opportunity for the Client to have second thoughts. Also, CM is often employed for design/build projects which inevitably incur a good many changes or modifications to the work. Many of these changes will be originated by the

Construction Manager whose task it is to integrate the work of multiple Contractors and to lessen the impact of conflict at interfaces. A Change Order is the easy way of accommodating elements that have been missed either from the drawings or the scopes of work. Because it is anticipated that all parties may flag a requirement for change, it is necessary to have a document that starts the process of identifying, costing and approving the change. For this purpose we have the Request For Change (RFC) which is described below.

REQUEST FOR CHANGE

As previously mentioned, Construction Management is a technique suited to and often used for design/build projects. In order to keep the project moving, all groups (managers, contractors, inspectors, consultants, etc.) are urged to operate as a Team and to cooperate in pin-pointing any missing elements or faulty interfaces.

To speed any correction required, all players are urged to prepare a "Request for Change" (RFC). This is a form that describes perceived errors or missing work and suggests that a Change Order be issued. Most RFCs will originate in the supervisory and inspection staff of the Construction Manager but **everyone** is encouraged to follow the procedure. The RFC is passed to the CM Project Manager who verifies the need and proceeds as for a Change Order.

> There was a builder who would not make any changes until all the work included in the original contract was completed. It usually happened that, by that time, the Client had either changed his/her mind or the expense and destruction involved was too great to contemplate. Needless to say, this requirement was justified by a clause in the contract - the average Client believes he/she knows what he/she wants when the contract is signed. The Builder assured me that he made very few changes.

CONSTRUCTION MANAGEMENT

"Construction Management" refers to the discipline or **profession** of the management of construction. In other words, the employment by a Client of a manager or management company on a fixed or variable **fee** basis to conduct all the functions of the Client, in respect of construction, on behalf of the Client, employing individual contractors by direct contract between the Client and the Contractor. The public and some contractors generally misunderstand the implications of this management methodology but it seems that the Client often prefers it because:

- it gives the **appearance** of a known ultimate cost, at the same time as
- an apparent assurance of the quality that the Client wants
- the Client has direct access to all the accounting (cost control)
- it eliminates some of the profit motive that the Client believes drives most contractors - this reassures the Client of an honest job

also see "Quality Assurance" (pg. 105)

To comment on the four points above:
- the project usually costs more than anticipated because the Client has more freedom to change his or her mind - a costly exercise
- quality assurance usually costs a lot more than the Client is prepared to pay or the Construction Manager is prepared to acknowledge
- true, but can the Client really appreciate its on-going significance?
- because of the potential for Client-initiated changes, there still is a chance for extra profits, perhaps not for the CM but for the trade or contract package contractors

Nevertheless, construction management (CM) is a sound methodology if carried out by a professionally-oriented Project Manager (and Team). The obvious and important difference (and problem) in the employment of **construction management** techniques is that there is no "General Contractor" as a functioning contractor to fill the gaps potentially left between trade contractors nor to take care of problems caused by poor workmanship (workpersonship?) that might affect a following trade.

It is a clause of most construction sub-contracts (and this applies equally to "contract package" contractors) that typically *"commencement of the work by this contractor implies acceptance of existing conditions as being suitable for proper performance of the work of this trade (or this contractor)"*. In a system where each contractor is independent of all others engaged on the project and, if one or more contractor has valid reasons for not commencing, then the schedule of work is immediately in jeopardy. And so is the budget: this contractor and all the following trade or package contractors may be in a position to make a claim for delay.

In respect of filling that gap between **trade** contractors (or **General Contractors** if the project is large enough to employ several) it is never wise and often specifically prohibited for the CM to perform such work directly. In the first place, if the CM does undertake construction work, it arouses suspicions in the mind of the Client and it also jeopardizes the professional attitude that the CM is demonstrating.

This problem of filling the gaps also holds true in normal general contracting practice but the General Contractor (GC) invariably has the resource capacity (his/her own construction staff and equipment) to fill any gaps or to remedy any defects in the work. The fact of being a GC also weighs heavily with Sub-contractors who realize that they can be quickly replaced if they default either by temporary workers of the GC or by the cancelling of their contract for "cause". In normal general contracting the Client (Owner) is more remote from them as they do not hold a contract **directly** with the Client but with the General Contractor.

The threat to the trade or package contractor is less under CM because cancellation of their contract is usually a protracted procedure requiring discussion and negotiation between the Client and the CM (remember that all the contracts are in the name of the Client - the CM merely **manages** them). So, bridging gaps caused by failure to maintain schedule and quality targets is not so simple when the Client holds all the contracts and acts through a professional Construction Manager. Unless the Construction Manager has let a contract to provide "Miscellaneous Services" he/she is unable to respond quickly to a requirement for missing construction elements except by issuing a Change Order to a contractor currently engaged on the project. An obvious corollary of this is that careful planning, constant revision of the schedule and meticulous inspection are essential to maintain momentum and to avoid cost overruns. If the Client does not choose a competent CM, then the Client is in deep trouble, deeper than with a General Contractor. *See below "Quality Control".*

QUALITY CONTROL

The **accepted** reason for quality control requirements is that it is what the Client wants and (theoretically) that is what the Construction Manager or General Contractor wants. A **practical** reason for proper control of quality when contracting by Construction Management methods is that the problems of coordination are greater under this system and poor workmanship or errors of execution are more difficult to correct; at the same time, they must not be allowed to delay the project. So, we may say that Construction Management imposes a more compelling requirement for quality control, for prompt and meticulous inspection at a level of detail that a General Contractor (erroneously) may not consider necessary.

GENERAL CONTRACTOR AS CONSTRUCTION MANAGER

General Contractors frequently are employed within a fee structure to perform as Construction Managers (CM). When this happens it is not unusual that the imperatives of normal contracting have previously governed the CM's staff to the extent that they tend to forget their new or temporary status as consultant professionals. It is essential to adopt a professional "attitude" when functioning as a CM; it is not easy to make this shift if one has spent years in a supervisory capacity pushing the trades for a General Contractor.

What is the difference? You may believe that there is no difference but, under CM, the traditional concern of the **professional** for the Client's needs, especially quality of performance, becomes more important than finishing the project in double-quick time in order to reduce overheads and increase profits.

There is nothing disparaging or abusive in this recognition of what drives General Contractors. They are in business to make a profit. Unnecessary time spent on a project is money lost and shareholders disappointed. A CM, on the other hand, is generally **guaranteed** a profit, in the form of a fee. Most often it is a fixed fee. So there is a certain impetus to perform quickly but still not the pressure experienced by a GC.

FEE STRUCTURE

The primary elements of a CM fee reimbursement structure are generally as follows:
1   fixed stipulated fee
2   salaries and benefits of a designated supervisory and inspection staff
3   reimburseable expenses in accordance with approved invoices

Seems simple enough - but of course it isn't. The main problem is that the major component of this fee structure is the cost of personnel. So what often happens is that the Client tries to persuade the CM to keep staff to a minimum. The CM compromises in order to get the contract and thereby both Client and CM jeopardize the effectiveness of the operation from the outset. A great deal more staff is required for the CM methodology than for normal general contracting.

Inadequate or inappropriate staffing will destroy a Construction Management project

A successful CM has to make the point strongly and persuasively - and justify it - that sufficient **qualified** staff is the primary pre-requisite for success. My own preference is for Project Supervisors or Coordinators plus the perhaps old-fashioned idea of a Clerk of Works for each trade - several as required for each trade on a big project. If the CM is experienced in this type of operation, there should be historical evidence to prove the need. Starting with insufficient staff is a guarantee of failure to some degree or other - and usually to a substantial degree.

It is difficult to stipulate detailed staffing requirements in general terms because of the variation in projects. However, as a guideline, the greater the variety of trades engaged, the more staff required; the more sophisticated the construction techniques, the more staff required; the more compressed the time schedule, the more staff required. A worst-case scenario could be a fast-track, design/build project in a location with extremes of climate.

Under these conditions, the CM could not:

- be sure initially of what materials would be employed because design is incomplete (how many different trade inspectors? - what should be their qualifications?)
- prepare with certainty a schedule of staff employment because of dependence on design progress
- even be **absolutely** sure of either milestone or overall completion due to a combination of weather problems and dependency on the design team
- be sure, under **any** conditions, of obtaining necessary Client approvals to ensure maintaining the schedule.

One recourse for the CM is to negotiate a fixed fee that would compensate for schedule overruns and the possibility of having to reinforce staff without full reimbursement - this will not appeal to the Client. Better yet, negotiate an open-ended staff roster that permits flexible hiring as needed, with full compensation for salaries and benefits; it would be necessary to prove each requirement to the Client but that should not be a problem for a reasonable Client (though you may think "reasonable Client" a contradiction in terms). In fact, almost every fee structure is difficult to negotiate and will ultimately prove unsatisfactory to the CM.

CONFLICT WITHIN CONSTRUCTION MANAGEMENT

There is a likelihood of conflict related to quality control (QC) within the CM organization in the same way as in General Contracting between the Contractor and the Designer. That is, the Managers or Supervisors responsible for coordinating and expediting the project may find that quality control appears to be an impediment to rapid completion of the work. First, we can say with assurance that this is not true. It may be that QC **appears** to delay the work but it ensures **proper** completion of the project; it avoids delays; it avoids cost overruns; it avoids having to re-do work.

Experience suggests that failure to recognize this potential for conflict is frequent and damaging to the project. So it is essential that the organizational structure of the CM be designed during the planning period to avert the problem. It is necessary that the reporting (hierarchical) arrangements be such that differences between branches of CM staff can be either eliminated or resolved quickly. The following chart (**figure 20**) is a recommended organizational structure that ensures there is an authority controlling all activities at a proper level for conflict resolution. Any arguments between "Quality Control" personnel (Inspectors, Clerks of Works) and the "Operations Supervisors" *(pushers)* will be referred back to the Project Manager for resolution. While it must be part of the job description of the Operations Supervisors that they maintain the standards required by the contract documentation, there is inevitably a natural tendency to recruit personnel for these positions from a field that supports speed over the niceties of finish.

figure 20

CONSTRUCTION MANAGEMENT ORGANIGRAM

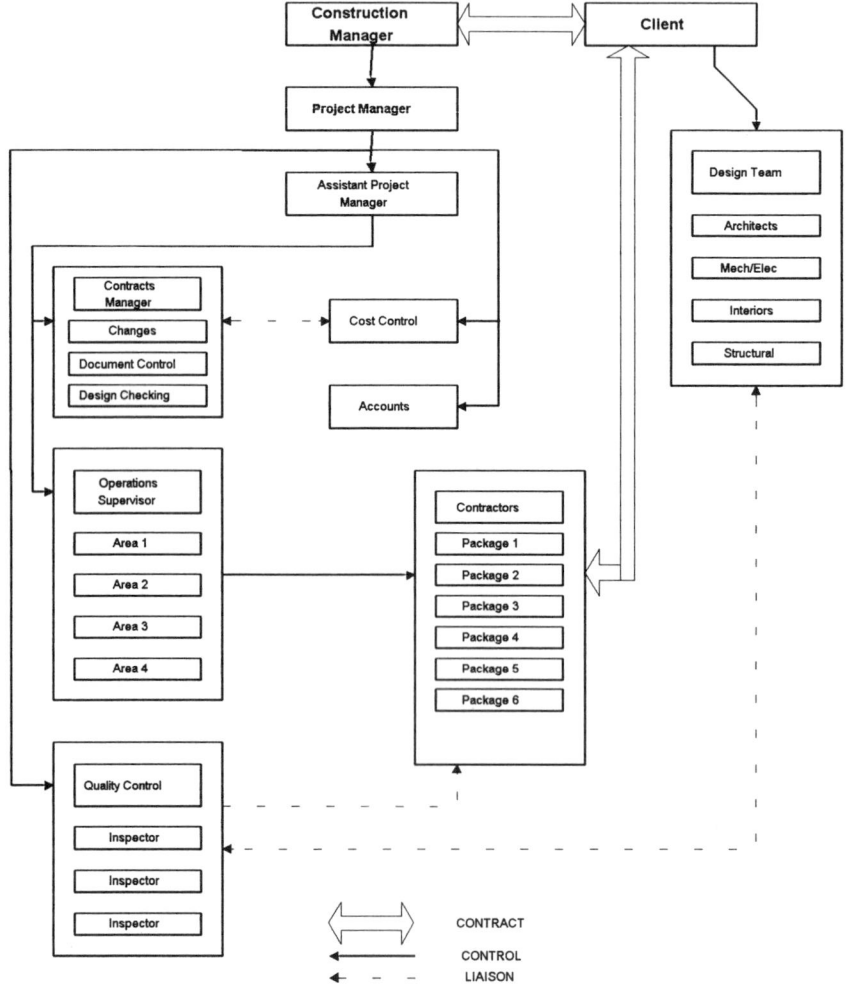

Note: there is a standard, understood requirement for communication between all the bodies controlled by the Construction Manager.

This organigram has been simplified to demonstrate the principle of separate units for Supervision and Quality Control. A complete chart indicating the breakdown of contract packages and the inter-merging of quality control between the packages would obscure the message.

Note, in respect of what was said in the introduction to this chart, that "Quality Control" is shown as reporting to the Project Manager, while "Operations Supervisor(s)" report to the Assistant Project Manager. The reason is that the Assistant Project Manager will be under a great deal of pressure to complete the project and will soon identify with the "Operations Supervisory" staff. Theoretically, the Project Manager (PM) will be the cool, calm, objective manager at a level concerned with the integrity of the total project. The PM should be able to remove him/herself from the natural conflict between "Operations" and "Quality Control". This is not to disparage either of the lower level staffs. Natural enthusiasm for their work objective tends to obscure for both of them the imperatives of the other group.

CONSTRUCTION MANAGEMENT AND THE SMALL BUILDER

There is no reason why a small Builder, a one-person business, should not offer construction management services. The principal components are the fee structure and the professional attitude to the work. The probable requirement for additional supervisory staff time applies equally but can be satisfied by the Builder accepting that he/she will be obliged to spend more time on the site ensuring precise coordination and the highest quality standards. Nevertheless, CM is not likely to be popular for small projects because the Client must enter into individual contracts with all the trade contractors; this would be more than a little intimidating for your average Client. Managing those contracts on behalf of the Client is also much more trying and time-consuming than the usual Builder/ Sub-trade relationship.

The small Builder may, by all means employ construction management techniques if you have an eminently reasonable Client who is anxious to obtain a perfect installation and who, while considering cost important, will not permit it to be the most important criterion. And, if you find that Client, please notify the author!

QUALITY ASSURANCE

The three parameters that best measure the success of any project are:

QUALITY   **TIME**   **COST**

They are all important and they are also interdependent. If, as the project proceeds, it is exceeding the budget (costing more than it should at intermediate milestones) then quality tends to deteriorate. The same thing applies if the project is behind schedule (if milestone completion target dates are not met).

The order of importance of the parameters (quality, time, cost) is dictated by the Client's priorities. These priorities tend to change during the progress of the work. Initially, quality is all important; later, when schedule becomes difficult to maintain, time assumes a greater importance. Ultimately for most Clients, cost is or becomes the most important criterion.

However, the Construction Manager or Builder/Contractor has an obligation to meet all of these parameters to the best of his/her ability. For the General Contractor, there is often a contractually imposed penalty should any of the parameters not be achieved within the terms described in the contract documents. The penalty for the CM is the fact that the fee is fixed no matter how much time is spent in getting it right - too much time eats up the fee and the profit.

There are some other potential adjustments (trade-offs) if all three parameters are not met:

♦ if **quality** is less than it should be, the Client may accept a discount or rebate to compensate for the loss - *a loss to the GC or to the Subs*
♦ in the case of an overrun of the **schedule,** there may be a per diem cash penalty deducted from the contract price for a GC which logically will be passed on to the Sub-contractor(s) responsible for the delay
♦ for a General Contractor, if the project **costs** more than the agreed contract price, then the GC loses that money. The GC will try to impose that loss on the Subs (trade contractors). The CM, on the other hand, is secure against that specific loss because the losses are for individual contractors, all of whom are directly contracted by the Client. The CM is acting in a **professional** capacity, so his/her most important incentive is to maintain a reputation for bringing in projects on time, on or under budget and of a quality acceptable to the Client. This is the way it **should** be.

DEFINITION

How do we define quality assurance (QA)? Perhaps as **"total compliance with the contract documents in respect of design and material use"**. In other words, the standards are established or are supposed to be established by the Client through the contract documentation. Obviously there can be large variations in quality standards depending on the Client's requirements. Of course there are basic minimums established by codes, regulations, material manufacturers standards and the standards of performance set by professional organizations (architects, engineers). Quality is the most difficult of the three basic parameters of success to define in a way that everybody understands and agrees.

To a large extent quality is a subjective consideration. The Client and Designer rarely see the same object in exactly the same manner as a Project Manager, Construction Manager or a Builder/Contractor.

> The Architect usually has a different perspective than either the Client or the Engineer. And an Engineer sees things differently to the Architect; his priorities are not the same - he wants it to stand up. The Architect wants it to look good as well as stand up. The Client wants it to perform a function; if there is a General Contractor (GC), he wants it to be all of these things and still make a profit. The Construction Manager has the same aspirations as the GC but, his profit is assured (though maybe smaller) and he must also consider maintaining his/her professional reputation.

There are **some** measurable quality parameters that can be evaluated mechanically. A simple example; the amount of water mixed with aggregate and cement to produce concrete. This is easily measured at the mixing plant; the question then arises as to whether it is still the same when it is placed; which we know can depend on how far from the plant to the site; how it is placed; how it is handled after it is placed and so on. It can, of course, be verified that the proper strength has been achieved by assessing the strength of the concrete from a sample taken at the pour and later by core samples taken from the cured concrete.

But there is no satisfaction and little value to either the Client or the CM or Builder in learning, 28 days later, that the concrete does not meet the strength standards. Concrete that fails a test may be accepted if it is not critical in a structural context or it may have to be broken out. The really important consequences - **delay and additional cost.**

In fact, if the Client or the Architect believes that the value of the project justifies the expense, there are specification descriptions that can dictate the minutest measurable details. For instance, moisture content of a concrete block wall can be determined before paint primer is applied; the thickness of the coats of paint may be specified and measured. Anyone who has seen the specs for a government project will have some idea of the detail that the experts can think up. How many painters know the ideal thickness of a coat of paint? Do I?

So the value of quality control through all stages of construction is obvious and so are the implications of not achieving the desired standards.

What are the fundamental requirements for good quality control?

♦ a set of proper contract documents - *they establish quality standards*

- for the **Construction Manager,** a professional attitude - the willingness of the Construction Manger to ensure that the work is performed correctly - *it is easier to dissemble [cheat, if you prefer] in construction than almost any other industry*
- for the **Builder/Contractor,** the integrity that is understood as an integral part of the agreement with the Client
- the **ability** of the inspection personnel to assess the performance of the work
- the certainty of the professional and moral **integrity** of the inspection personnel - *skilled, honest and resolute inspection personnel are essential to the success of a quality control program*
- for the **Construction Manager**, a budget sufficient to provide all the required expertise
- for the **Builder,** a carefully calculated estimate that allows for adequate supervision an, equally important, meticulous selection of competent Sub-contractors.

In order to make all these things happen, certain organizational and procedural conditions are essential with particular emphasis as shown below:

Quality Assurance for the Construction Manager

Typically, the Construction Manager must ensure that he/she has:
- a proper contract for the Client/Trade or Package Contractor relationship
- a proper contract for the Client/Construction Manager relationship
- a practical organization structure that embraces all the players in the project
- job descriptions that make clear the functions of each element and their interrelationships
- well-qualified, experienced, positive, honest personnel
- a management that has:
  the **capacity** to select inspection staff
  the **will** to support inspection staff
- an early and continuing review of the contract documents as they are prepared
- procedures for the imposition of the authority of the Construction Manager
- procedures for the integration into the quality assurance cycle of all organizational elements that have a legitimate interest in the success of the project such as:

  * Construction Manager   * Authorities having jurisdiction
  * Client   over the project
  * Designers   * Contractors and/or sub-contractors

Quality Assurance for the Builder/Contractor

Because quality assurance is vital to the success of any project no matter what the management method and because quality work is the best recommendation for future projects, the differences between the Construction Manager and the Builder are more administrative than fundamental. So the Builder/Contractor needs:

- a proper contract for the Client/Contractor relationship
- a proper contract for the Contractor/Sub-contractor relationship
- a practical organization structure that embraces all the players in the project
- job descriptions that make clear the functions of each element and their interrelationships - or a clear understanding of what those functions are
- well-qualified, experienced, positive, honest personnel
- competent management
- a clear understanding, based on the forms of contract, of the authority of the Contractor
- clearly understood or written procedures for the integration into the quality assurance cycle of all organizational elements that have a legitimate interest in the success of the project such as:
    * Contractor personnel
    * Client
    * Designers
    * Authorities having jurisdiction over the project
    * Sub-contractors

Quality Assurance for CM and General Contractor

The CM and General Contractor must be sure of:
- unimpeachable plans and specifications
- an implementation schedule that establishes inspection requirements

Quality Assurance for Client and CM

The Client may need some persuading but it is preferable that the CM be employed sufficiently early to assist the Client in the review of the contract documents. This is particularly important in design/build projects (for which CM is logically favoured) as the CM is able to guide the development of the design and construction documents in the most economical progression from the point of view of economies in construction techniques and scheduling. The development of contract packages is extremely difficult for this type of project and, without close cooperation between designers and Construction Manager, many additional costs may be incurred, in particular because of interface problems between packages and building elements.

COST OF QUALITY ASSURANCE

Quality Assurance (QA) usually costs more than anticipated but not usually more than it **should** cost if it is properly done. I have said before that it is usually **undervalued** in respect of the savings it can bring at all project stages. All design and construction procedures are traumatized by the general disinclination to spend money on good organization up front rather than spending it putting things right after the fact.

Spend money to *avoid* mistakes, not in *correcting* them

It is unfortunate but no surprise to most Builders that, typically, the Client tries to get the Designers on the cheap. The Client tries to beat down the Contractor's bid. The Contractor does the same to his/her Sub-contractors. Consequently, the Designers and the Contractor try to save money on inspection and supervision. Unfortunately, it is well nigh impossible to establish a real basis for trust in this industry. The nature of the game is that projects are short term - just long enough to decide whether or not the relationship is a good one ..... and then it is all over.

Effective quality control begins with the design. The Client must be prepared to give the designer a fair deal so that he/she can produce adequate documentation. The Designer is entitled to expect that; the Builder would be surprised were it to happen.

Quality of work improves directly relative to the comprehensiveness of **effective** quality control. At the same time, the **apparent** completion schedule may extend in a similar relationship to what **appears** to be an increase in quality control. Nevertheless, proper quality control will always keep overall cost within budget for the Client and the Construction Manager and the Builder. What is more, the project will still achieve its **realistic** completion date.

There is altogether too much unreal optimism in the setting of schedules; this really does nothing for the progress of the project, upsets the Client when targets are not met and creates a similar unreality in respect of all the financial aspects of the project. The competent Project Manager must know what is a realistic target for completion, must know how to manage his/her resources to make it happen, must know how to overcome the passing crises that always occur and must be able to meet not only schedule but quality imperatives within the budget. It is not easy being a Project Manager. It is even more difficult to be a successful one.

PERSONNEL QUALIFICATIONS

It has already been suggested above that the standard of QA will be a direct product of the standard of the personnel inspecting and supervising the work.

Remember, also, that **nobody** is completely reliable.

There is no offence in checking someone's work; there is no shame in having one's work checked by another. In fact, job descriptions should be worded so it is obvious that this will be done.

> When I was an apprentice junior engineer still in my late teens, I made a 30 cm. (12") error in setting the height of a brick-built manhole (it may be a person-hole now; it was a manhole then!). The manhole was some 4 metres square and the wall 20 cms. thick. Luckily I discovered the error before anyone else. At 1:00 a.m. the following morning, I took a 4lb. hammer and a cold chisel and toiled till dawn, chipping off the top 4 courses of bricks and burying them in the sand around the MH. I was a very tired junior the next day but a much more careful one in future.

Experience is the primary requirement for good inspection capability. You can study and learn about construction but the long-time tradesman can tell at a glance what is wrong with a piece of carpentry, a plumbing joint, an electrical connection, whether a painted wall has one, two or three coats. Your typical Clerk of Works used to be a bit long in the tooth, steady, unflappable, incorruptible and knowledgeable. Do they still exist? If you find one, hang on to that person.

FACTORY INSPECTIONS

It is not a usual requirement of inspection that the Builder/Contractor visit a factory, fabrication plant or shop to inspect work that is to be incorporated into the project. It should be done more often. A considerable amount of time and money may be saved by avoiding unnecessary deliveries of materials that do not fit the specifications or the dimensions. No-one is immune to error (I may have said this before). Consider a factory inspection as an effort to assist the manufacturer. If you think such an inspection will be required, make sure it is included as an item of the purchase order or contract.

Shop drawings are good, shop inspections are better

The size or cost of the project has nothing do to with this requirement. How many times have windows or cabinets or miscellaneous metals been delivered to the site only to be found in error? Once on the site, it is difficult to get them off again - no matter what the contract says. This usually means either accepting the work as it is, altering it on site (unsatisfactorily) or adjusting someone else's work to accommodate it. Everybody loses time and money.

EXECUTION

> **DURING EXECUTION**
> - follow the Plan
> - make adjustments to the plan to suit changing conditions
> - **supervise and inspect the work carefully**
> - anticipate problems
> - communicate effectively
> - acquire information that will simplify evaluation

To some Builders everything that has been described about planning may seem an unnecessary waste of time. They are "dirty boot" entrepreneurs, love to be on the site directing operations, seeing something grow before their eyes. This is a great feeling and, if all you want to do is fulfil your dream to build the biggest sand-castle, that's fine. If you want to succeed and grow as a Builder, then you must get used to the dull bits as well. Planning may be the most boring but it is the most important phase of your operations.

Planning is boring
Orderly execution is boring

Now we come to the other tiresome part; executing or implementing the project in an **orderly** manner. This means keeping up with the paper-work, coordinating the participants, making sure everyone performs properly, reviewing the progress of the work, keeping the Client up to date on what is happening, ensuring compliance with the contract documents, maintaining a proper cash-flow, ensuring quality and a thousand and one other activities.

COORDINATION

Coordination requirements are established in the planning stage of the project - the Plan of Operation. When the **Organigram** is prepared, it indicates obvious requirements for coordination of the bodies or trades shown on the chart. The execution **schedule** takes this a step further and can be used to show the details of interfaces between the contributors to the project. Complex projects require more sophisticated techniques because there are more interfaces between trades, more breaks in operations, tighter control of material deliveries and so on.

Time to warm up the computer and develop a network diagram (PERT is the most common). There are so many software packages available (I just counted 60 in a listing of useful programs) and such frequent improvements (improvements?) in software that it is impossible to make recommendations. If you are a company large enough to need computer technology, you probably already have a system in place.

The small operator should be wary of embarking on the use of a computer for coordination or scheduling purposes; it is easy to end up spending more time before the screen than on the site!

also see Section 3, Project Planning,"Schedule" (pg. 48)

INTERFACES in Program Environments

Interfacing of project elements within the project is critically important but equally important is the interfacing of the project with the project environment. Coordination takes on a new dimension when other projects are involved or contingent on this one. This applies to your own (company) work program as well as the environment of other parties involved either directly or peripherally in the project.

also see Section 3, "Coordination & Interfaces" (pg. 88)

If some part of this environment is, for instance, a government organization with all its bureaucratic implications of departments, rules and regulations, political imperatives, etc., a **program** of many inter-connected projects potentially will have interfaces between component projects and the overall program - of which your project may be a small part.

In such cases, consideration must be given, during your project planning, to the organizational framework into which the planned project must fit and steps must be taken to ensure that it continues to progress properly within that environment during execution and as an operational element when the project is successfully completed *(interface of project with operational entity)*. All of this interaction may have been previously anticipated and planned by the Client but the impacts on your project depend on the skill with which this planning was done - something over which, under these circumstances, you have no control.

Therefore, the PM should try to make him/herself aware of the operational structure of not just the project but the total organization of which it will become a part. Should there be uncertainty as to the final format into which the project must fit (a certainty if you are working for government), the PM must devise an assumed but logical framework based on his/her own knowledge of political and hierarchical constraints and the requirements of the project. Do this in such a way that the inevitability of your proposed structure will be so apparent as to make it easily acceptable to Client and/or authorities or that, at least, the proposed interfaces will be recognized as necessary or, failing that, provide a basis for discussion of these interface problems. So:

- always plan for project interfaces that may occur
- always plan organizational interfaces
- try to be aware of final operational interfaces
- always take into account program/project interfaces
- if operational and program interfaces have not been flagged, make rational assumptions for Client acceptance and approval - *if the Client thinks you are an interfering busybody poking your nose into what does not concern you, accept this with good grace and do not say "I told you so" when some other operation is delayed because of uncontrollable problems with your project.*

SUPERVISION

Defined in the dictionary as "to have oversight of, to oversee or superintend", supervision includes the following activities - and a good many more:

- implementation of planning and scheduling
- coordination of the Sub-trades
- co-ordination of your own staff
- definition and monitoring of interfaces
- ordering of materials and equipment
- being available to answer queries
- ensuring safety on the site
- keeping the site clean and orderly
- ensuring compliance with building codes and regulations
- interpretation of contract documents (plans, specs., shop drawings, etc.)
- assessing the requirement for a change (sometimes assessing its cost)
- anticipating requirements for and calling for inspections as required
- ensuring that the paperwork is up-to-date, including written reports
- maintaining a log of progress to assess payments to Subs and progress claims from the Client
- ensuring compliance with the budget
- keeping a project diary
- inspection of the work (quality assurance)
- maintaining amicable relationships with Client and/or Consultants

If you are a one-person Builder, you will have to do all these things and many more yourself. Bigger companies have appropriate staff for special duties. But the Project Manager is responsible for ensuring that all activities happen as they should.

also see Section 3, Project Planning, "Supervision" & "Inspection"

> Reflections on Supervision
> Is there a Builder (or a Client) who has not heard "But we always do it that way!"? The tradesman who cannot be bothered to read the plans or thinks there is no time to ask a question or just doesn't give a dam makes this an excuse for faulty work. Some examples:
> - a house garage door was designed off-centre to permit a structural bracing at one side; the framer installed the door dead centre although the drawing was dimensioned. The reason: "We always put the garage door in the centre!"
> - a winding staircase had to pass under a beam; the designer went to the site, drew the location of every tread and riser on the wall. When the work was inspected, it was impossible to walk under the beam. Why the change? "We always do it that way!"
> - a kitchen counter-top was designed and meticulously drawn with a 4 foot long section 5 inches lower to permit easy dough-making; it arrived and was installed at the standard height. The reason? You guessed it!

INSPECTION

Inspection is treated in this manual as an activity distinct from "supervision", although often performed by Supervisors. It refers to ensuring the detail of compliance with the contract document requirements in the sense of accuracy and quality. For instance, an early site inspection requires that you check the setting out of the building. If it has been done by a surveyor, verify a few of the dimensions. Check a couple of diagonals to make sure it is square where it should be. Do you think this is not necessary? Have you never found a wrong dimension after the building is completed? - and had to confess it to the Client or invent a reason? Nobody is immune to error (what, again?); and that includes the Surveyor and you, the Builder/Project Manager. Large builders may employ engineering staff to lay out the project but an occasional check on their work will be beneficial.

> *If you do not already know it, an easy way to check for squareness (90 degree angle) is to measure a multiple of 3 along one side, a multiple of 4 along the other and the diagonal will be a multiple of 5. (The old 3,4,5 trick.) You can achieve a surprising accuracy with two steel tapes and two people.*

Inspection during execution (construction) does not mean simply looking at the **quality** of the work on the site or the adherence to the schedule. It is necessary, at each inspection first to review that part of the contract documents that concerns the element you are inspecting. Before leaving for the site or immediately upon arrival, look through the drawings and specifications.

Review the documents before you check the work

If you are checking the cabinet work, for instance, make sure you know what finish is required on the doors, what colour is the counter-top - does the installation match the sample? (Surprising how often this is wrong). Is there supposed to be a caulking bead at the floor, or at the top of the splashback. Make sure that a bulkhead above wall cabinets is installed if required. If you are anticipating the delivery of the cabinets, has the floor covering been protected before they are brought in.

> *Do not believe that the specified colours will necessarily be the ones supplied. In a Federal public building in Ottawa, two huge changing rooms were tiled from floor to ceiling with the wrong coloured ceramic tile. They were ripped out and replaced after a struggle of wills between the GC and Sub on one side and a very tough Clerk of Works on the other. We know that under pressure to complete the work, Subs have been known to go with what they have rather than be delayed - and hope that no-one will notice or the General Contractor or Client will be steam-rollered into acceptance.*

On larger buildings, inspection is obviously more complex. A favourite omission, for instance, is "openings" in poured concrete beams. There is an incredible amount of money and time wasted, not to mention embarrassment suffered, because the Contractor has to return to the Engineer for advice on penetrating a beam. Avoiding this means a careful study of both the structural **and** the mechanical and electrical drawings before the pour is made. Do not leave this inspection to the last minute. If your structure is heavily reinforced, you may have to delay work to allow changes to the steel. As often as not, openings in beams are shown as an "x" in a box on a 1:100 (1/8" scale) drawing with no location dimensions - not surprising they are often missed.

An important aspect of this sort of inspection problem and the need for reviewing the contract documents first is the question of **responsibility** for error. Take the example above. Who is responsible for setting out the openings in beams? Is there a clear assignment of responsibility in the specifications, in the Scope of Work, or in the individual contracts of the various trade sub-contractors involved? Is there an obligation on the part of the formwork Sub to check with the mechanical? Is that responsibility clearly indicated in the contract documents? Usually, the structural engineer will have coordinated this aspect with the mechanical engineer during design but this **frequently** does not happen or changes are made afterwards without advice to the other engineer.

Who then is responsible? It may be considered a design error but generally there is a catch-all clause in the construction contract that puts the onus on the General Contractor. The General in turn passes that on to a Sub-trade. Rather than wasting a lot of time after the fact trying to assign responsibility, spend the time up-front looking for these possible errors and omissions. They are always there. No matter who carries the can when the blame is assigned in legal or contractual terms, **everyone** loses money and time (and, believe me, assigning financial responsibility is never as easy or as obvious as it should be). The extra cost may be covered by a contingency but, remember that contingency funds not disbursed are profits for the Builder.

Sometimes in inspection and supervision, it is difficult to see the wood for the trees. A hackneyed phrase but apt. Do not concentrate so much on one aspect of an inspection that you ignore the adjacent or associated elements. An example is, perhaps, the best illustration:

> As a Consultant, I was asked to check on the setting out of brickwork on a large one-storey residential building. The Contractor was a perfectionist and I was required to ensure that the "brickie" had every horizontal joint equal in thickness in order to finish at the soffit of the ring beam, already poured. This was done by the bricklayer, myself following every move with great care and unsurpassed attention to detail. The next day, the Contractor called me and asked what had happened to the doors. The bricklayer foreman and I had been entering and leaving the building through full-height windows, had devoted ourselves exclusively to the accuracy of the brickwork and the "brickie" had built right across the doors. And we had watched him do it! If you are immune to this sort of error, you may have a good laugh at my expense.

All this diligence in searching documents, in apportioning responsibility and making the culprit pay may give the impression that an inspector has to be tough and hard-nosed. Right. A Project Manager, in either a management or inspection role, must never expect to be popular; the P.M.'s Team must never expect to be popular. The members of the team responsible for inspection might be pleased to be nothing more than **un**popular! As an independent Builder or a Building company, you are imposing contractual obligations on Sub-contractors and suppliers; do not expect them to be always well-disposed toward you. Ask nothing more of them than the contract legally requires; perform your part properly and you can have the satisfaction of knowing that you have been **fair**. After all your first duty is to your Client who is entitled to a proper contract fulfilment.

As a Builder, you will also have to deal with other people's inspectors, Client or Consultant or authority having jurisdiction over the project (municipalities, code regulators, etc.). They will or should spend a great deal of time reviewing the contract documents and ensuring compliance. This is another reason for you to be as diligent as they are. Find the loopholes or inconsistencies as soon as you can. Bring them to the attention of the authority; make proposals for changes if necessary and indicate costs and delays that might be incurred. Do this **in writing**. Try not to be caught out - be one step ahead.

Review the applicable contract documents before inspection
Review the contract documents during inspection

PROJECT COMPLETION

There are several complex and tedious procedures involved when a project finishes. The difficulty and aggravation depends on the complexity of the project and there is likely to be more of both the bigger the project and the more Sub-contractors involved. Projects with a large mechanical and electrical component are probably the most troublesome.

COMMISSIONING

Different types of projects terminate in different ways but "termination" or "completion" occurs at a specific milestone and is a specific activity; the amount of work involved depends on the type and size of the project.

As an example, a building, an Education Centre, must be known to **function** before title is transferred or confirmed. This particular aspect may or may not be of concern to the Builder in a legal sense but it may affect the date on which the project can be considered **completed.** To ensure the acceptability of the installation, each responsible party must complete its activities, be seen to complete them and have them declared satisfactory. For instance:

- the mechanical Sub-contractor tests all equipment in the presence of the inspector and the Project Manager (PM)
- the Architect, with the PM and the Client, inspects all construction and installations
- incomplete work is noted and scheduled for future completion (see below)
- insurance policies are reviewed for compliance and outstanding claims
- the Architect confirms that all changes have been recorded on the drawings (probably it is the Builder's responsibility to record the changes)
- equipment warranties and manuals are assembled and handed to the Architect or the Client
- assurance of compliance with local authority and other government

regulations is obtained and recorded
- keys are handed to the Client (if all other conditions have been fulfilled as certified by the Architect - lien terms, deficiencies, incomplete work, etc.)

Activities similar in consequence, if not in character or extent, govern the termination of all projects; the nature of the project as it develops through the Plan of Operation will make it clear what the special requirements are for each project. For any project, simple or complex, it is better if the Plan of Operation makes it clear what the requirements will be.

figure 21

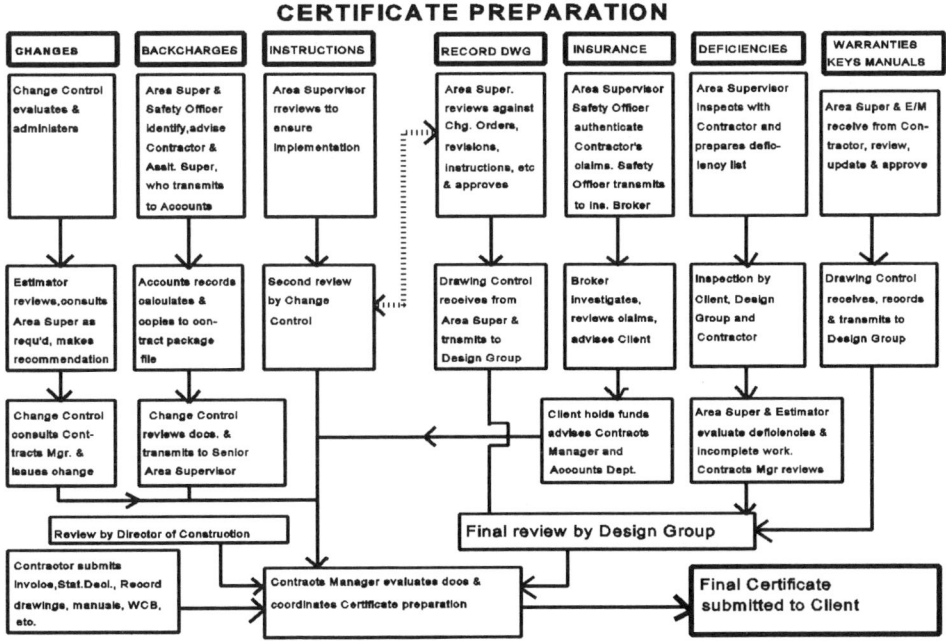

The chart above was used on a large project executed using Construction Management techniques (the contracts were all in the name of the Client rather than the Construction Manager). It was a "design/build" project completed to schedule (by the grace of God). It illustrates some of the activities that have to be completed to justify the authorization of the "Final Certificate" of payment.

Note the 7 important activities that had to be known to be completed and note the complex inter-coordination necessary to arrive at a condition that the Architect and Client would agree as suitable for acceptance and authorization of final payment.

The activities are:
- Changes - *change Orders have a financial and scheduling implication*
- Back-charges - *if any have been forgotten, you will never recover the money*
- (Site) Instructions - *many will have been reflected in the Change Orders; make sure none were missed*
- Record Drawings (as-builts) - *the Architect must accept them*
- Insurance - *all claims must have been settled or authorized*
- Deficiencies - ***see below***
- Warranties/Keys/Manuals - *it sometimes takes months to get the manuals!*

*Note that the **procedures** dominate the activity flow rather than the contributors. The procedures required to complete the contract are the headings of each block of activities (e.g. "Back-charges" which are claims by the Client against individual contractors). The activities that govern the procedures flow from box to box, following the arrows. Departments and individuals occupy the boxes wherein those activities are registered. Nevertheless, it is comparatively easy for those individuals to trace their activities through the chart and to determine at what point they are involved and what action is required of them. The departments and individuals involved in this procedure include: Change Control (Contacts Management Department); Area Supervisors; Senior Area Supervisor; Safety Officer; Contractor; Assistant Superintendent; Accounts; Estimator; Drawing Control; Insurance Broker; Design Group; Electrical/Mechanical (E/M); Director of Construction; Contracts Manager, Client, etc.*

This was a large public works project with numerous interested "parties" making a detailed Procedures Manual essential. The chart did not attempt completely to replace the project Procedures Manual but, given that the information it contains was set out elsewhere in detail if reference were required, the chart provided a quick check to ensure that all activities were being performed in the proper order - and it was a lot easier to read than the manual. It is often better to summarize activity flows on a chart rather than to leave people to plod through long descriptions. Fortunately, most projects are not this complex but it illustrates the need for **anticipation** of all those activities that are required for successful completion or termination.

DEFICIENCIES AND INCOMPLETE WORK

A "deficiency" is something that has been done badly. "Incomplete Work" is something that has either not been done or not been completely done. An inspection for deficiencies and incomplete work is usually performed when the Builder supposes the work to be "substantially complete". The usual game is for the Builder to claim "completeness" as early as possible and for the Client or

Consultant to deny it as long as possible. The reasoning is obvious as a lot of money is involved in confirming "completeness" (completion, termination).

Naturally, there is often disagreement between the parties involved as to what is the status of the work. The Architect, Engineer or other Consultant is the expert and is supposed to display a professional impartiality in making decisions on doubtful elements. It would seem simple enough to decide what is incomplete, not quite so easy to determine what is deficient. Unfortunately it is never that easy. On a large project, two, three, four and sometimes more inspections are required before agreement is reached. Don't forget that the Architect has the last word. If he or she refuses to consider the project as complete, the only recourse is to the terms of the contract - generally arbitration but sometimes the courts. It would have to be a powerful disagreement for things to get to that stage but it happens.

Strictly speaking, only the Architect and the Builder are required to perform a deficiency inspection. Usually the Client wants to get in on the act - after all, it is his or her money! This is very annoying for the Builder but difficult to avoid. Clients have an irrational desire for something more than they are prepared to pay for and the Builder is sure that no-one could have done the work better. The Architect or designer is in the middle - so, before you get mad at the Architect for being so picky, try to see it from his/her point of view.

VALUATION OF DEFICIENCIES

In order to make a disbursement at substantial completion, the work will often be accepted with deductions for incomplete work and deficiencies - providing they are not excessive. The Architect has the right to stop the inspection if he or she considers the work to be below an acceptable level. The rational Builder does not allow this to happen as it puts the Architect one-up and makes it difficult to persuade the Architect to schedule another inspection. The fewer "final" inspections the better for all concerned. The more re-inspections, the more picky becomes the Architect; if you irritate the Architect, he or she can always, quite justifiably, find **something** wrong.

It is usual to value incomplete work at the actual cost of doing the work and deficiencies at twice the cost. The reasoning has logic; work not done cannot be worth more than its actual value while deficiencies means correcting work, maybe tearing it down and rebuilding, which must cost more. Both parties have to agree on the valuations but the Architect has the edge. Expect a lot of debate about costs.

Deficiencies and Sub-contractors

A well-planned and well-executed project, run by a competent Project Manager, will anticipate deficiency inspections and the need for some corrective work. An efficient, well-organized Builder will have scheduled inspections with the Sub-contractors. The ideal is that the Builder and the Sub (one trade at a time or several together whose work impinges on each other) make an inspection when the Sub considers the work complete and the Builder agrees in principle. All the comments above in respect of the project apply to the work of each Sub-contractor. Deficiencies and incomplete work must be taken care of. Payments will not be made until corrections have been carried out.

A Builder who does this will be in a position to waltz the Architect through the project in double-quick time, knowing that everything has been taken care of. This is extremely good for the Builder's reputation and of some considerable benefit to his or her ego. It does not happen often.

Also the Project Manager/Builder is entitled to stop the inspection any time that things are found that are clearly inadequate. However, if this happens, it is equally clear that there has been a lack of proper inspection by the Project Management staff during the execution of the work. Do not allow this to happen.

Deficiencies in Construction Management

All of the above observations apply equally to Construction Management (CM) projects but there is the additional hazard that, because of the usual application of CM to design/build or similar projects, many of the Contractors may be long gone and paid off when the total project or program is inspected for completion and final payment. For this reason, contractor final inspections (package contracts or trade contracts) must be infinitely more meticulous and rigorous. The potential for the later impact of unnoticed deficiencies on following contractors (still working on the project) must be taken into account. There is little recourse against the contractor who has gone except by insurance and bonding - an additional cost.

Back-charges

The Certificate Preparation chart (**figure 21** - pg.119) has an activity listed as Back-charges; this will be a familiar term to most builders. In essence it is simple enough. In the relationship between Client and Builder and more frequently in the relationship between Builder and Sub-contractor, where there is some negligence on the part of the one who is being paid by the other, then the one paying may deduct payment for the alleged negligence.

For instance, a Sub-contractor who damages another Sub's work can be "back-charged" the cost of repairing the damage. If a Builder backs his or her truck into the Client's house, the Client may deduct the cost of the repairs from the Builder's next payment. That is an extreme example; obviously, the Builder would repair the damage and, in any case is covered by insurance. But there are many obscure delinquencies that are not observed until the project is near completion or actually completed especially in the Builder/Sub-contractor relationship.

Damage to another Sub's work may not be discovered until the Sub at fault has completed his/her work; in this case, the deduction would be made from the "holdback". Major incidents do not often occur but, on a large project, failure to clean up debris by a dozen or so trades can cause substantial delays and impose costs on either other Subs or the General Contractor. For which reason, all incidents that may merit a back-charge should be recorded in the project diary and be immediately brought to the attention of the wayward contractor. Back-charges should not be allowed to accumulate. They are always contentious; if they are not billed as interim payments are made but are allowed to build up to a substantial sum, there will surely be a disagreeable confrontation when the deduction is made. So, advise the Sub-contractors of delinquencies as they are observed and inform them as soon as possible thereafter of the cost. More paperwork, it is true, but less trouble later.

> On a multi-storey, construction management project in Ottawa, the trade contractors steadfastly refused to clean up their rubbish. The CM had little recourse because it was often difficult to decide which Sub was responsible. The solution: the CM employed 4 motor-cycle club members as "clean-up crew". They (all 1200 lbs. of them) "suggested" to the Subs that the "clean-up crew" would be much happier if the Subs did not leave debris around. The site was near spotless within a week.

FOLLOW-UP

It is not enough to plan something, to issue an instruction that something be done, to order a material or a service without also ensuring that what you expect to happen actually does. This is all part of supervision and organization but as an important element of project management technique requires a special mention.

FOLLOW-UP - CATEGORY 1

Always follow up **in writing** on any points that have been mutually agreed between parties or individuals, especially those points that may have a contractual implication. This should be a natural consequence of communication at a meeting (the minutes) but in one-on-one discussions it is equally important. A judgement call is required as to what is sufficiently important to be committed to paper but the Project Manager is required to recognize this criterion in all his or her activities; it is something that must be instinctive in your management skills. If the agreement or variation does not merit a Change Order, a Site Instruction or even a memorandum, at least make sure that it is entered in the project diary.

    Contracts, in which changes are recognized as being a natural consequence of the agreement, require a standard format for changes to be noted and approved. In construction generally, first a Site Instruction then a Change Order or Variation Order and in CM sometimes a Request for Change (RFC) as a first action.

also see Section 4, "Change Order", "Site Instruction" (pg. 98)

FOLLOW-UP - CATEGORY 2

More vigorous, more aggressive follow-up is often required in order to ensure that events unfold as they should. As an example, an order has been placed or the attendance of an expert requested and delivery or compliance has been promised for, let us say, a date three weeks ahead. One week beforehand, telephone to remind the supplier or expert of the date. Three days before delivery is due, call again to make sure that your reminder has not been forgotten and that all the details are correct. Then, on the day previous to the critical date, check again to ensure that the delivery time is established, that the proper address for delivery is known or the location of the site is not in doubt; give any final information. This persistent follow-up applies equally to shop-drawings, to documents to be provided by a Consultant, as it does to equipment or materials contracted to be supplied.

If you are prepared to believe that written follow-up ("Follow-up, Category 1") will tend to irritate people, you can imagine that **this** will drive them crazy. However, it gets results. The number of reminders required and the amount of irritation that needs to be applied depends on circumstances but, in all projects, some degree of motivation is required to make things happen.

FOLLOW-UP - CATEGORY 3

Just as vital, but most often neglected, is the follow-up on activities or events that are not necessarily required to be reported back immediately to the Project Manager (PM) or which may not have an immediately visible effect.

A typical case for a small project - an instruction is given to a Sub-contractor for remedial work to be performed on a project that, supposedly, has been completed. A period during which the remedial work will be performed is established.

Apart from any reminders to the Sub-contractor during that period (depending on the time lapse), the Project Manager will check with the Sub-contractor on the day following planned completion of the correction. On receiving the expected assurance that the work has been done, the PM then calls the Client to verify that complete satisfaction has been received. If not, then the whole process must start again but with more aggression on the part of the PM.

Assuming that all this process was carried out by telephone (reasonable in the case of small works or minor activities, quickly performed) now is the time to confirm the requirement in writing with a vigorous expression of dissatisfaction at failure properly to execute both the original work and the correction. Other than repetition of the follow-up, the steps beyond this are, of course, referral to the contract requirements and the possibility of the imposition of contractual penalty clauses, warranties, bonding agents and so on - if those are terms of the contract.

This particular project management activity rarely receives its due attention; follow-up is important at all levels of activity. There are usually several persons between the sufferer of neglect (the Client) at the bottom end of the service and the Project Manager at the top. Make sure that staff understand the necessity of following-up and reporting back.

The Project Manager dare not assume that everything will fall into place; nor should he/she assume that the responsible party in charge will follow up as he/she should. Frequent reminders are justifiable for everybody in this remedial process in order to ensure that the final action is soundly based and timely.

> My first task as Contracts Manager on a large Public Works project was to persuade a contractor to complete some remedial work that should have been done 3 weeks before. I immediately sent a telegram saying that, if the work were not commenced within 24 hours, another contractor would complete it and the responsible contractor would be back-charged. The contractor complained to the Minister, the Deputy Minister, the Senior Project Manager and the janitor. I was told not to send any more telegrams .... but the work was begun next morning as instructed. You will have times like this.

FOLLOW-UP - CATEGORY 4

Equally important as follow-up of **action** is follow-up and communication of **inaction**. It is important that, if there is a break in some anticipated course of events, some uncompleted activity, a delay, a cancellation, that everyone engaged on or concerned with the project be aware. Make sure that the Sub-contractors, the Client and others involved know **what** is not happening, **why** nothing is happening and **when** the inaction should end. Just as it is more difficult to find what is missing from a contract than to establish what is included, so it is more difficult to determine what actions are missing rather than what actions have been performed - either properly or improperly. So keep on top of the problem.

DEALING WITH CONSULTANTS

It is advisable to establish a good relationship with Architects, Engineers and other Consultants. Be agreeable but do not be subservient; know the contract documents as well as they do; be absolutely fair in complying with their requirements. Expect no more than you are entitled to; give what is called for to the best of your ability. Some professionals assume a greater authority than should be theirs and get away with it because they wield a lot of power - they control the disbursement of money.

Do not let them take you for granted. A contract is an agreement between two parties; your rights are the equal of the Client's and the consultant is merely the

Client's agent. Respect the Consultant for his or her abilities but do not allow yourself to be bullied - but be polite in all your dealings with them.

Treat the Architect with respect but do not be bullied

Make all your submissions, whatever they are, on time in the proper format and without deception. If you are claiming a progress payment or estimating a Change, make sure you can justify all your figures. If you have to fight with the Architect every time you present a Change Order or a payment claim because they are either inaccurate or exaggerated, you will be losing time that were better spent on a **real** management activity. You can save a lot of management time by building a reputation for accuracy - consultants will get to know you and that you are reliable.

also see Section 4, "Change Orders" (pg. 160)

CONTROL

Good control starts with good planning (*see Section 2, Planning, "Control"*) If you have an inadequate contract or even worse, no written contract, your control of the project is already jeopardised. It is essential that the Project Manager and his/her Team be in **control** of the project throughout its duration (on behalf of the Client, of course). The importance of control in all stages of project management cannot be over-emphasized. The Project Manager should control planning as well as execution (implementation), completion, evaluation terms and warranty management. As a Builder, you prepare your own Plan of Operation; this Plan tells you how to execute the project, evaluate and administer the warranty. In other words, it all depends on starting with a Plan.

CONTROL CRITERIA

The most important control criteria are:
- detailed planning - *in order to know what is happening it is essential to know what* **should** *be happening*
- phasing or staging - *a project should be broken down into manageable, measurable pieces*
- milestones - *stages or phases should be defined by* **clearly-described** *naturally-occurring milestones*
- commitment - *the "Team" (this means both management and Sub-contractors) must be totally supportive of the project objectives and the management philosophy*

- interfacing - *obtain prior compliance by agreement or by contract from all concerned in all interfaces*
- monitoring - *all the participants and their activities are subject to close overview at all times; supervision and inspection must be properly planned, adequately budgeted and* **meticulously done**
- measurement data, properly planned, make monitoring easy and effective
- communication - *failure to communicate all actions to all Team members and the Client (or the Client's agents) jeopardizes control*
- leadership - *the Project Manager must:*

    * guide the Team
    * communicate
    * make essential decisions
    * reduce conflict
    * appraise and reward effort
    * reflect the requirements of the Client

The Builder is the Leader - communicate to maintain control

EVALUATION

There was a brief mention of the need for and the principles of Project Evaluation in Section 2. A thorough evaluation can be complex if the long term effects of the project and its success are considered. But here are some of the questions that should be asked to provide you with answers as to the **immediate** success of the project and to suggest ways that you may improve your techniques for the next project. Take the principal elements of your Plan of Operation.

BUDGET

Were expenditures at the various milestones correct? Were additional payments required to some Subs? Were they required because of poor drawings or poor descriptions of the work? Did the Client pay on time? Were the payments sufficient to keep your cash-flow positive on this project?

ORGANIGRAM

Did you have more bodies on the project than you anticipated? If so, who were they and why were they needed? Did Consultants create any problems - slowing the work schedule or requiring more than you bid for? Did you have to change the organigram during the project and, if so, why?

WORK BREAKDOWN STRUCTURE

Did the break-down as you planned it answer all your requirements? Did you miss something at any of the various levels? Was the Work Breakdown Structure (WBS) too detailed (you must know where to draw the line)?

> I had bid on several projects for a certain architect and failed to win any of them. I determined to make a perfect estimate for the next one I bid. I made an incredibly detailed WBS and material list; I priced every item on the list including such things as running feet of quarter round and the number of cuts and mitres required. Each item was meticulously priced. Some readers will know what happened. My estimate was astronomical. I learned then that common sense is just as important as attention to detail!

SCHEDULE

Were all your milestone dates met? Did your Subs arrive on the site when they should? Did you complete on schedule? And if not were your overheads greater than they should have been? If your Subs were late, was it because you didn't keep them informed or didn't remind them (again and again) when they were due to start?

CONTRACTS

Have you had any problems with the type of contract you are using? **Is anyone suing you?** And if not, were you just lucky?

CONTRACT WARRANTIES

Did you provide the Client with all the written warranties to which he or she is entitled? Are you sure that all your Subs and suppliers can and will honour their warranties? Have you sufficient funds to monitor the warranties, yourself if they let you down?

LOGICAL FRAMEWORK ANALYSIS

If you are using the Logical Framework Analysis (LFA), were your "Critical Assumptions" justified? Were there some that you missed? In other words, did you anticipate all the difficulties you might encounter?

SECTION 4

DOCUMENTS

Unfortunately, it is not possible to run a project without paper - a lot of paper. Most builders hate paper-work and a lot of them suffer financially because they neglect it - perhaps for neglecting as little as one page or one paragraph of written instructions. If you want to be successful, you must get used to the idea that a lot of administration is necessary. If you cannot afford to employ someone to do it for you, you must do it yourself. "Builders and Contractors" who are not prepared to be meticulous with their paper might as well give up. I put that in inverted commas because you are neither a complete Builder nor a complete Contractor if you can't face the tedium of administrative work.

**Paper-work is a necessary part of the
Builder and Contractor's work**

CONTRACTS

The Contract between the Builder and the Client is the one that has most significance for the Builder. It is also the most neglected, especially by the "small" builder. Because a contract, for the Builder, is simply an agreement between parties to perform work for a specific reimbursement, it **may** be done with no paper-work at all if both parties are willing and both have a complete understanding of their obligations. No intelligent Builder would risk this - not even for his or her mother!

So, how much paper is required? Is it sufficient to write on the back of your business card *"I will build your house for $200,000.00?"* Not many people would think that it is. But most Builders and, for that matter, most Clients do not want 30 pages of fine print. Where to draw the line?

My belief is that, it is always best to press for the form of contract sponsored by the professional bodies that represent builders, contractors and professionals. In Canada the common one is the format of the Canadian Construction Documents Committee (CCDC), representing Contractors, Engineers and Architects. They have a format for each typical construction contract.

There will be occasions when this will seem an exaggeration from any viewpoint and as an alternative I suggest the Proposal form also included in this section. It is usually sufficient for **small alteration or renovation** work. There really is very little between the two options that is either more suitable or acceptable. Abstracting or eliminating parts of the CCDC contract is not a good idea. Unless you are a lawyer, you will end up removing something that turns out to be the most important clause of the original. The document that follows is based on the CCDC format and is recommended for general use for a "stipulated price" or "lump-sum" contract. The fact that it has a good many clauses that do not apply to your project is of no consequence; better to have too many than too few - you just ignore the ones that do not apply.

Believe it or not - the lawyer is the Builder's best friend!

No matter what form of contract you use, you should always have it checked by your lawyer. For large contracts, have each individual contract reviewed; for smaller projects, get your lawyer to approve a simple standard format. Build a good relationship with your lawyer. Every business person will need a lawyer at some time.

Contracts are mostly "common-sense" in a legal format

STIPULATED PRICE

This is the most common form of contract; a specific amount of work to be performed for a specific sum in a specific time. There are clauses in the contract (General Conditions) that permit changes in the price (up or down) and changes in the time schedule.

Do not be overwhelmed by the amount of information included in this document. Most of it is just plain common-sense. Most of it you will be doing anyway. But it does eliminate most of the situations that cause arguments and litigation between contractors and clients. The contract that follows has been found useful but is not necessarily definitive.

STIPULATED PRICE CONTRACT

AGREEMENT BETWEEN OWNER AND CONTRACTOR (stipulated price contract)

This Agreement made in duplicate this twenty-third day of February 1995

by and between John and Mary Doe jointly and severally, hereinafter called the **Owner**, and Better Builders Inc., hereinafter called the **Contractor**,

witnesseth: that the Owner and the Contractor undertake and agree as follows:

A-1 **THE WORK**

The Contractor agrees to:

a) perform all the Work required by the contract documents for additions to the property known as 3830 Carlington Street, Victoria which were prepared by Victoria Associates on behalf of the Owner, acting as and hereinafter called the Designer and

b) do and fulfil everything indicated by this Agreement, and

c) commence the work within one week of receiving the Contract Documents or sooner at the discretion of the Contractor and, subject only to adjustment as provided for in the Contract Documents, attain Substantial Performance of the Work, being *completion of all drywall installation*, as mutually agreed by the Owner and Contractor, within *sixty (60)* working days of commencement of the Work, except as shall be otherwise agreed in writing between the parties.

A-2 **CONTRACT DOCUMENTS**

The following is an exact list of the Contract Documents referred to in Article A-1 of this Agreement and as defined in item 1 of DEFINITIONS. This list is subject to subsequent amendments in accordance with the provisions of the Contract and agreed upon between the parties. Terms used in the Contract Documents which are defined in the attached DEFINITIONS shall have the meanings designated in those definitions.

    1   this Agreement
    2   General Conditions
    3   Supplementary General Conditions
    4   Description of the Work as contained in the *"Proposal" by the Contractor dated February 2, 1995*
    5   Drawings provided by *Victoria Associates*
    6   any subsequently agreed amendments or changes to the Contract.

A-3 **CONTRACT PRICE**

In consideration of the performance of the Work, the Owner agrees to pay the Contractor in *Canadian funds the amount of forty-five thousand, four hundred and ninety two dollars ($45,492.00)*, which price shall be subject to adjustment as may be required in accordance with the General Conditions of the Contract.

A-4 PAYMENT

(a) Subject to applicable legislation and the provisions of the Contract Documents, and in accordance with legislation and statuary regulations respecting hold-back percentages, the Owner shall:

1. make a first payment to the Contractor of *twenty thousand dollars ($20,000.00)* within five (5) days of the signing of this contract.
2. make a second payment of *twenty thousand dollars ($20,000.00) within 15 days* of Substantial Performance of the Work, which shall be construed as the completion of the installation of all drywall.
3. make a final payment of *five thousand four hundred and ninety-two dollars ($5,492.00)* on the completion of the lien period, that is forty-one (41) days following Total Performance of the Work which is agreed as *the completion of the installation of carpet.*

(b) In the event of loss or damage occurring where payment becomes due under the property and boiler insurance policies, payments shall be made to the Contractor in accordance with the provisions of GC 20 - INSURANCE.

(c) If the Owner fail to make payments to the Contractor as they become due under the terms of this Contract or in an award by arbitration or court, interest of *two percent (2%)* per month, *twenty-six point eight percent (26.8%)* per annum on such unpaid amounts shall also become due and payable. Such interest shall be calculated from the date of the first default and added to any unpaid amounts on a bi-weekly basis.

A-5 RIGHTS AND REMEDIES

(a) The duties and obligations imposed by the Contract Documents and the rights and remedies available thereunder shall be in addition to and not a limitation of any duties, obligations, rights and remedies otherwise imposed or available by law.

(b) No action or failure to act by the Owner, Designer or Contractor shall constitute a waiver of any right or duty afforded any of them under the Contract, nor shall any such action or failure to act constitute an approval of or acquiescence in any breach thereunder, except as may be specifically agreed in writing.

A-6 RECEIPTS OF AND ADDRESSES FOR NOTICES

Communications in writing between the parties or between them and the Consultant shall be considered to have been received by the addressee on the date of delivery if delivered by hand to the individual or to a member of the firm or to an officer of the corporation for whom they are in*tended or, if sent by post or by telegram, to have been delivered within* five (5) working days of the date of mailing, dispatch or of delivery to the telegraph company when addressed as follows:

The Owner at: 3830 Carlington Street
Victoria,
B.C. Canada

The Contractor at: 2000 Vampire Avenue
Victoria, B.C. Canada

A-7 LAW OF THE CONTRACT

The law of the Place of the Work shall govern the interpretation of the Contract.

A-8 LANGUAGE OF THE CONTRACT

At the request of the parties hereto, the language of the Contract shall be English.

A-9 SUCCESSION

The General Conditions of the Contract hereto annexed, and all the other aforesaid Contract Documents, are to be read into and form part of the Agreement and the whole shall constitute the Contract between the parties and, subject to law and the provisions of the Contract Documents, shall enure to the benefit of and be binding upon the parties hereto, their respective heirs, legal representatives, successors and assigns.

In witness whereof the parties have executed this Agreement under their respective corporate seals and by the hands of their proper officers thereunto duly authorized.

SIGNED, SEALED AND DELIVERED
in the presence of:

Owner   Witness

John Doe
name

_____
signed

Mary Doe   Witness
name

_____
signed

Contractor

Better Builders Inc.   Witness
name:

_____
signed

GENERAL CONDITIONS OF THE CONTRACT

GC1 DEFINITIONS

1.1 Contract Documents

The Contract Documents consist of the executed Agreement and the General Conditions of the Contract, Supplementary General Conditions, Specifications where applicable, Drawings, and such other documents as are listed in Article A-2 of the Agreement including all amendments thereto incorporated before their execution and subsequent amendments thereto made pursuant to the provisions of the Contract or agreed upon between the parties.

1.2 Owner, Consultant, Contractor

The Owner, Consultant where applicable and Contractor are the persons, firms or corporations identified as such in the Agreement and referred to throughout the Contract Documents as if singular in number and masculine in gender. The term Owner, Consultant and Contractor means the Owner, Consultant and Contractor or their authorized representatives as designated by each party in writing.

1.3 Subcontractor

A Subcontractor is a person, firm or corporation having a direct contract with the Contractor to perform a part or parts of the Work included in the Contract, or to supply products worked to a special design according to the Contract Documents, but does not include one who merely supplies products not so worked. Wherever the singular number and masculine gender occur, plural number and feminine gender apply where the facts or contents so require.

1.4 The Project

The Project is the total construction of which the Work performed under the Contract Documents may be the whole or a part.

1.5 The Work

The term "The Work" means the total construction required by the Contract Documents and includes all labour, products and services.

1.6 Products

The term "Products" means all material, machinery, equipment and fixtures forming the completed Work as required by the Contract Documents but does not include machinery and equipment used for preparation, fabrication, conveying and erection of the Work and normally referred to as construction machinery and equipment.

1.7 Other Contractor

The term "Other Contractor" means any person, firm or corporation employed by or having a separate contract directly or indirectly with the Owner for work other than that required by the Contract Documents.

1.8 Place of Building

The place of building is the designated site or location of the Project.

1.9 Law of the Contract

The laws of the place of building shall govern the contract.

1.10 Time

(a) The Contract Time is the time stated in Article A-1 (c) of the Agreement for Substantial Performance of the Work.
(b) The date of Substantial Performance of the Work is the date certified by the Consultant.

(c) The term "day" as used in the Contract Documents shall mean the calendar day.
(d) The term "working day" as used in the Contract Documents shall mean days other than Saturdays, Sundays and holidays which are observed by the construction industry in the area of the place of the building.

1.11 Substantial Performance
Substantial Performance is as defined in the Mechanic's Lien legislation applicable to the place of the building. If such legislation is not in force or does not contain such definition, or should there be no specific agreement to the contrary between the parties, Substantial Performance shall have been reached when the Work is ready for use or is being used for the purpose intended and is so certified by the Consultant.

1.12 Total Performance
Total Performance shall mean when the entire Work has been performed to the requirements of the Contract Documents and is so certified by the Consultant or as may otherwise have been agreed between the parties.

GC2   DOCUMENTS

2.1 The Contract Documents shall be signed in duplicate by the Owner and the Contractor.
2.2 The Contract Documents are complementary and what is required by any one shall be as binding as if required by all.
2.3 The intention of the Contract Documents is to include all labour, products and services reasonably necessary to perform the Work in accordance with these documents. It is not intended, however, that the Contractor shall supply any products or work not covered by or properly inferable from any of the Contract Documents.
2.4 Words which have well-known technical or trade meanings are used in the Contract Documents in accordance with such recognized meanings.
2.5 In the event of conflict between Contract Documents, the following shall apply:
(a) Documents of later date shall govern.
(b) Figured dimensions shown on the drawings shall govern even though they may differ from scaled dimensions.
(c) Drawings of larger scale shall govern over those of smaller scale of the same date.
(d) Specifications shall; govern over drawings.
(e) The General Conditions of the Contract shall govern over Specifications.
(f) Supplementary General Conditions shall govern over General Conditions of the Contract.
(g) The Agreement shall govern over all documents.

GC3   ADDITIONAL INSTRUCTIONS

3.1 During the progress of the Work the Consultant shall furnish to the Contractor such additional instructions as may be necessary to supplement the Contract Documents. All such instructions shall be consistent with the intent of the Contract Documents
3.2 Additional instructions may include minor changes to the Work which affect neither the Contract Price nor the Contract Time.
3.3 Additional instructions may be in the form of drawings, samples, models or written instructions.
3.4 Additional instructions shall be issued by the Consultant with reasonable promptness and in accordance with any schedule agreed upon.

GC4 DOCUMENTS PROVIDED

4.1 The Contractor shall be provided, without charge, with as many copies of the Contract Documents or parts thereof as may be reasonably necessary for the performance of the Work.

GC5 DOCUMENTS ON THE SITE

5.1 The Contractor shall keep one copy of all current Contract Documents and shop drawings on the site in good order and available to the Consultant and/or his/her representative. This requirement shall not be deemed to include the executed Contract Documents.

GC6 OWNERSHIP OF DOCUMENTS AND MODELS

6.1 All Contract Documents and copies thereof, and all models furnished by the Consultant are and shall remain his/her property and are not to be used on other work.
6.2 Such documents are not to be copied or revised in any manner without the written authorization of the Consultant.
6.3 Models furnished by the Contractor or the Owner are the property of the Owner

GC7 CONSULTANT'S DECISIONS

7.1 The Consultant, in the first instance, shall decide on questions arising under the Contract Documents and shall interpret the requirements therein. Such decisions shall be given in writing. The Consultant shall use his/her powers under the Contract to enforce its faithful performance by both parties thereto.
7.2 The Contractor shall notify the Consultant, in writing, immediately should he/she hold that a decision by the Consultant is in error and/or at variance with the Contract Documents.
7.3 If the question of error and/or variance is not resolved immediately, and the Consultant decides that the disputed work shall be performed, the Contractor shall act according to the Consultant's written decision. Any question of change to Contract Price and/or extension of Contract Time due to such error or variance shall be decided as provided in GC16 - Settlement of Disputes.
7.4 Should the Consultant's employment be terminated, the Owner shall appoint a Consultant whose status under the Contract shall be that of the former Consultant.
7.5 Nothing contained in the Contract Documents shall create any contractual relationship between the Consultant and the Contractor.

GC8 DELAYS

8.1 If the Contractor be delayed in the performance of the Work by any act or neglect of the Owner, Consultant or Other Contractor or any employee of any one of them, then the Contract Time shall be extended for such reasonable time as the Consultant may decide in consultation with the Contractor, and the Contractor shall be reimbursed for any cost incurred by him/her as the result of such delay.
8.2 If the Contractor be delayed in the performance of the Work by a Stop Work Order issued by any court or other public authority, and providing that such order was not issued as the result of any act or fault of the Contractor or anyone employed by him/her directly or indirectly, then the Contract Time shall be extended for such reasonable time as the Consultant and the Contractor may agree that the work was delayed and the Contractor shall be reimbursed for any costs incurred by him/her as the result of such delay.
8.3 If the Contractor be delayed in the performance of the Work by labour disputes, strikes, lock-outs (including lock-outs decreed or recommended for its members by a recognized Contractor's Association, of which the Contractor is a member), fire,

unusual delay by common carriers or unavoidable casualties or, without limit to any of the foregoing, by any cause of any kind whatsoever beyond the Contractor's control, then the Contract Time shall be extended for such reasonable time as may be mutually decided by the Consultant and the Contractor, but in no case shall the extension of time be less than the time lost as the result of the event causing the delay, unless such shorter extension of time be agreed to by the Contractor..

8.4 In addition and without limit to the foregoing, the Contract Time may be extended for any cause within the Contractor's control which the Consultant shall decide as justifying a delay for such reasonable time as the Consultant may decide.

8.5 No extension shall be made for delay unless written notice of claim is given to the Consultant within fourteen (14) days of its commencement, providing that in the case of a continuing cause of delay only one claim shall be necessary.

8.6 If no schedule is made under GC3 - Additional Instructions, no claim for delay shall be allowed on account of failure to furnish instructions until two (2) weeks after a demand for such instruction and not then unless such claim is reasonable

8.7 The Consultant shall not, except by written notice to the Contractor, or as provided in GC15 - Emergencies, stop or delay any part of the work pending instructions or proposed changes to the Work.

GC9   OWNER'S RIGHT TO DO THE WORK

9.1 If the Contractor should neglect to prosecute the Work properly or fail to perform any provisions of the Contract, the Owner, subject to the approval of the Consultant, may notify the Contractor in writing that he/she is in default of his/her contractual obligations and instruct him/her to correct the default within five (5) working days of receiving the notice.

9.2 If the correction of the default cannot be completed within the five (5) working days specified, the Contractor shall be considered to be in compliance with the Owner's instruction if he/she:
   (a) commence the correction of the default within the specified time, and
   (b) provide the Owner with an acceptable schedule for such correction, and
   (c) completes the correction in accordance with the schedule.

9.3 If the Contractor cannot comply with the provisions of 9.1 and 9.2, the Owner may, without prejudice to any other right or remedy he/she may have, correct such default and may deduct the cost thereof from the payment then or thereafter due the Contractor provided, however, that the Consultant shall approve both the action and the amount subsequently charged to the Contractor.

GC10   OWNER'S RIGHT TO STOP WORK OR TERMINATE CONTRACT

10.1 If the Contractor should be adjudged bankrupt or make a general assignment for the benefit of creditors or if a receiver be appointed on account of his/her insolvency, the Owner may, without prejudice to any other right or remedy he/she may have, by giving the Contractor written notice, terminate the contract.

10.2 Subject to the receipt of a certificate from the Consultant verifying that sufficient cause exist, the Owner may notify the Contractor in writing that he/she is in default of his/her contractual obligations, if the Contractor:
   (a) refuse or fail to supply sufficient properly skilled workers or workmanship, products or construction machinery or equipment for the scheduled performance of the Work within five (5) working days of receiving written notice from the Consultant, except in those cases provided in GC8 - Delays; or,
   (b) fail to make payments due to his/her Subcontractors, suppliers or workers; or,
   (c) persistently disregard laws or ordinances, or the Consultant's instructions; or,
   (d) otherwise violate the provisions of the Contract to a substantial degree.

Such written notice by the Owner shall instruct the Contractor to correct the default within the five (5) working days from the receipt of the written notice.

10.3 If the correction of the default cannot be completed within the five (5) working days specified, the Contractor shall be considered to be in compliance with the Owner's instruction if he/she:
   (a) commence the correction of the default within the specified time, and
   (b) provide the Owner with an acceptable schedule for such correction, and
   (c) complete the correction in accordance with the schedule.
10.4 If the Contractor fails to correct the default within the time specified or subsequently agreed, the Owner may, without prejudice to any other right or remedy he/she may have, by giving written notice, stop the Work or terminate the contract.
10.5 If the Owner terminate the Contract under the conditions set out in GC10 above, he/she is entitled to:
   (a) take possession of the premises and products and utilize the construction machinery and equipment, the whole subject to the rights of third parties, and to finish the Work by whatever methods he/she may deem expedient but without undue delay or expense.
   (b) withhold any further payments to the Contractor until the Work be finished;
   (c) upon Total Performance of the Work, charge the Contractor the amount by which the full cost of finishing the Work as certified by the Consultant, including compensation to the Consultant for his/her additional services and a reasonable allowance as determined by the Consultant to cover the cost of any corrections required by GC33 - Warranty, exceeds the unpaid balance of the Contract Price; or if such cost of finishing the Work be less than the unpaid balance of the Contract Price, pay the Contractor the difference.

GC11 CONTRACTOR'S RIGHT TO STOP WORK OR TERMINATE THE CONTRACT

11.1 If the Owner should be adjudged bankrupt or make a general assignment for the benefit of creditors or if a receiver be appointed on account of his/her insolvency, the Contractor may, without prejudice to any other right or remedy he/she may have, by giving the Owner written notice, terminate the contract.
11.2 If the Work should be stopped or otherwise delayed for a period of thirty days or more under an order of any court, or other public authority, and providing that such order was not issued as the result of any act or fault of the Contractor or anyone directly or indirectly employed by him/her, the Contractor may, without prejudice to any other remedy he/she may have, by giving the Owner written notice, terminate the Contract.
11.3 The Contractor may notify the Owner in writing with a copy to the Consultant, that the Owner is in default of his/her contractual obligation if:

   (a) the Consultant fail to issue a certificate in accordance with GC23 - Certificates and Payments;
   (b) the Owner fail to pay the Contractor when due any amount certified by the Consultant or awarded by arbitrators.
   Such written notice shall advise the Owner that if such default not be corrected within five (5) working days from the receipt of the written notice, the Contractor may, without prejudice to any other remedy he/she may have, stop the Work and/or terminate the Contract.
11.4 Should the Contractor terminate the Contract under the conditions set out above, he/she shall be entitled to be paid for all work performed and for any loss sustained upon products and construction machinery and equipment with reasonable profits and damages.

GC12 OTHER CONTRACTORS

12.1 The Owner reserves the right to let contracts in connection with the project of which the Work is part.
12.2 The Owner shall coordinate the Work and insurance coverage of Other Contractors

as it affects the Work of this Contract.

12.3 The Contractor shall coordinate his/her work with that of Other Contractors and connect as specified or shown in the Contract Documents. Any change in the costs incurred by the Contractor in the planning and performance of such work which was not shown or included in the Contract Documents as of the date of signing the Contract, shall be evaluated as provided under GC21 - Valuation and Certification of Changes in the Work.

12.4 The Contractor shall report to the Consultant any apparent deficiencies in Other Contractors' work which would affect the Work of this Contract immediately they come to his/her attention and shall confirm such report in writing. Failure by the Contractor to so report shall invalidate any claims against the Owner by reason of the deficiencies of the Other Contractor' work except as to those of which the Contractor was not reasonably aware.

12.5 The Owner shall take all reasonable precautions to avoid labour disputes or other disputes on the Project arising from the work of Other Contractors.

GC13   ASSIGNMENT

13.1 Neither party to the Contract shall assign the Contract or any portion thereof without the written consent of the other, which consent shall not be unreasonably withheld.

GC14   SUBCONTRACTORS

14.1 The Contractor agrees to preserve and protect the rights of the Parties under the Contract with respect to any work to be performed under subcontract. The Contractor therefore agrees to:
  (a) require his/her Subcontractors to perform their Work in accordance with and subject to the terms and conditions of the Contract Documents, and
  (b) be as fully responsible to the Owner for acts and omissions of his/her Subcontractors and of persons directly or indirectly employed by them as for acts and omissions of persons directly employed by the Contractor.

The Contractor therefore agrees that he/she will incorporate all the terms and conditions of the Contract Documents into all Subcontract Agreements entered into with the Subcontractors.

14.2 The Contractor agrees to employ those Subcontractors proposed by him/her in writing and accepted by the Owner prior to the signing of the Contract for such portions of the Work as may be designated in the bidding requirements.

14.3 The Owner may, for reasonable cause, object to the employment of a proposed Subcontractor and require the Contractor to employ one of the other subcontractor bidders.

14.4 In the event that the Owner require a change from any proposed Subcontractor, the Contract Price shall be adjusted by the difference in cost occasioned by such required change.

14.5 The Contractor shall not be required to employ as a Subcontractor any person or firm to whom he/she may reasonably object.

14.6 The Consultant may, upon reasonable request and at his/her discretion, provide to a Subcontractor information as to the percentage of the Subcontractor's work which has been certified for payment.

14.7 Nothing contained in the Contract Documents shall create any contractual relationship between any Subcontractor and the Owner.

GC15   EMERGENCIES

15.1 The Consultant has authority in an emergency to stop the progress of the Work whenever in his/her opinion such stoppage may be necessary to ensure the safety of life, or the Work, or neighbouring property. This includes authority to make changes in the Work, and to order, assess and award the cost of such work, extra to the Contract or otherwise, as may in his/her opinion be necessary. The Consultant shall within two (2) working days confirm in writing any such instructions. In such a case if work has been performed under direct order of the Consultant, the Contractor shall keep his/her right to claim the value of such work, notwithstanding Article 1690 of the Quebec Civil Code, where this clause may apply.

GC16   SETTLEMENT OF DISPUTES

16.1 In the event of any dispute arising between the parties as to their respective rights and obligations under the Contract, either party hereto shall give to the other notice of such dispute within thirty (30) days of the occurrence. The requirement of the immediate notification of the circumstances provided for in GC7.2 shall not be considered to have been modified by the aforegoing time limitation.

16.2 In the event that the parties have agreed to submit such disputes to arbitration pursuant to a Supplementary General Condition of the Contract, or by subsequent agreement, either party may, to the extent that such an agreement permit, thereupon request arbitration pursuant to such provision.

16.3 In the event that no provision or agreement is made for arbitration, then either party shall have the right to seek recourse in such judicial tribunal as the circumstance may require.

16.4 In recognition of the obligation of the Contractor to perform the disputed work as provided in GC 7.3, it is agreed that settlement of dispute proceedings may be commenced by either party at that time.

GC17   INDEMNIFICATION

17.1 Except as provided in 17.2 and 17.3, the Contractor shall indemnify and hold harmless the Owner and the Consultant, their agents and employees from and against all claims, demands, losses, costs, damages, actions, suits, or proceedings arising out of or attributable to the Contractor's performance of the Contract, providing that any such claims, damage, loss or expense is:
   (a)   attributable to bodily injury, sickness, disease or death or to injury to or destruction of tangible property; and
   (b)   is caused by a negligent act or omission of the Contractor or anyone for whose acts he/she may be liable.

17.2 The obligations of the Contractor under this General Condition shall not extend to the liability of the Owner and the Consultant, their agents and employees where the primary cause of the injury or damage arises out of:
   (a)   the use of maps, drawings, reports, surveys, change orders, designs or specifications provided by the Owner, the Consultant, their agents and employees, or
   (b)   the giving of or the failure to give decisions or instructions by the Owner, the Consultant, their agents and employees.

17.3 The Owner shall indemnify and hold harmless the Contractor from and against all claims, demands, losses, costs, damages, actions, suits, or proceedings arising out of the Contractor's performance of the Contract which are attributable to lack of or a defect in title or an alleged lack of or defect in title to the site of the Work.

GC18   CONTINGENCY ALLOWANCE

18.1 The Contract Price includes all the cash allowances stated in the Contract Documents.

18.2 The contingency allowance is specified to provide for changes in the Work authorized under GC20 - Changes in the Work, and evaluated under GC21 - Valuation and Certification of Changes in the Work.

GC19   CASH ALLOWANCES

19.1   The Contract Price includes all cash allowances stated in the Contract Documents. In this contract the only cash allowance is an amount of one hundred and sixty-three dollars ($163.00) for the purchase of light fixtures.

19.2   Cash allowances, unless otherwise specified, cover the net cost to the Contractor of all services, products, construction machinery and equipment, freight, unloading, handling, storage, installation and other authorized expenses incurred in performing the work stipulated under the cash allowances.

19.3   The Contract Price, and not the cash allowance, includes the Contractor's overhead and profit in connection with such cash allowances.

19.4   Where costs under a cash allowance exceed the amount of the allowance, the Contractor shall be compensated for any excess incurred and substantiated plus an allowance for overhead and profit as set out in the Contract Documents.

19.5   The Contract Price shall be adjusted by written order to provide for any excess or deficit to each cash allowance.

19.6   Progress payments on account of authorized purchases under cash allowances shall be certified on the Consultant's monthly certificates for payment.

19.7   A schedule shall be prepared jointly by the Consultant and Contractor to show when items called for under cash allowances must be authorized by the Consultant for ordering purposes so that the progress of the Work will not be delayed.

GC 20   CHANGES IN THE WORK

20.1   The Owner, through the Consultant, without invalidating the Contract, may make changes by altering, adding to, or deducting from the Work, with the Contract Price and the Contract Time being adjusted accordingly.

20.2   Except as provided in GC 15 - Emergencies, no change shall be made without a written order from the Consultant and no claim for an addition or deduction to the Contract Price or change in the Contract Time shall be valid unless so ordered and at the same time valued or agreed to be valued as provided in GC 21 - Valuation and Certification of Changes in the Work.

GC 21   VALUATION AND CERTIFICATION OF CHANGES IN THE WORK

21.1   The value of any change shall be determined in one or more of the following methods:

(a) by estimate and acceptance in a lump sum;
(b) by unit prices set out in the Contract or subsequently agreed upon;
(c) by cost and a fixed or percentage fee.

21.2   When a change in the Work is proposed or required, the Contractor shall present to the Consultant for approval his claim for any change in the Contract Price and/or change in Contract Time. The Consultant shall satisfy him/herself as to the correctness of such claim and, when approved by him/her, shall issue a written order to the Contractor to proceed with the change. The value of work performed in the change shall be included for payment with the regular certificates for payment.

21.3   In the case of changes in the Work to be paid for under methods (b) and (c) of 21.1, the form of presentation of costs and methods of measurement shall be agreed to by the Consultant and Contractor before proceeding with the change. The Contractor shall keep accurate records, as agreed upon, of quantities or costs and present an account of the cost of the change in the Work together with vouchers where applicable.

21.4   If the method of valuation, measurement and the change in Contract Price and/or change in Contract Time cannot be promptly agreed upon, and the change is required to be proceeded with then the Consultant shall determine the method of valuation, measurement and the change in Contract Price and/or Contract Time subject to final determination in the manner set out in GC 16 - Settlement of

Disputes. In this case the Consultant shall issue a written authorization for the change, setting out the method of valuation and, if by lump sum, his/her valuation of the change in Contract Price and/or Contract Time.

21.5 In the case of a dispute in the valuation of a change authorized in the Work, and pending final determination of such value, the Consultant shall certify the value of work performed and include the amount with the regular certificates for payment.

21.6 It is intended in all matters referred to above that both the Consultant and Contractor shall act promptly.

GC 22 APPLICATION FOR PAYMENT

22.1 Application for payment on account as provided for in Article A-4 may be made monthly, or as otherwise agreed, as the Work progresses.

22.2 Application for payment shall be dated the last day of the agreed monthly payment period or other period and the amount claimed shall be for the value, proportionate to the amount of the Contract, of work performed and products delivered to the site at that date.

22.3 At the specific request of the Consultant, the Contractor shall submit to the Consultant before the first application for payment, a schedule of values of the various parts of the Work, aggregating the total amount of the Contract Price and divided so as to facilitate evaluation of applications for payment.

22.4 This schedule shall be made out in such form, and supported by such evidence as to its correctness, as the Consultant may reasonably direct, and, when approved by the Consultant, shall be used as the basis for application for payment, unless it be found to be in error.

22.5 When making application for payment, the Contractor shall submit a statement based upon this schedule. Claims for products delivered to the site but not yet incorporated in the Work shall be supported by such evidence as the Consultant may reasonably require to establish the value and delivery of the products. The Contractor shall cooperate in any inspections required by the Consultant, either at the Site or other storage location, to determine the delivery of the products.

22.6 Where applicable, applications for release of holdback monies following the Substantial Performance of the Work and the application for final payment shall be made at the time and in the manner set forth in GC 23 - Certificates and Payments.

GC 23 CERTIFICATES AND PAYMENTS

23.1 The Consultant shall, within ten (10) days of receipt of an application for payment from the Contractor submitted in accordance with GC-22 - Application for Payment, issue a certificate for payment in the amount applied for or such other amount as he/she shall determine to be properly due. If the Consultant amend an application, he/she shall promptly notify the Contractor in writing giving reasons for the amendment.

23.2 The Owner shall, within five (5) days of the issuance of a certificate for payment by the Consultant, make payment to the Contractor on account in accordance with the provisions of Article A-4 of the Agreement.

23.3 Notwithstanding any other provisions of this Contract:

(a) If on account of climatic or other conditions reasonably beyond the control of the Contractor, there are items of work that cannot be performed, the payment in full for work which has been performed as certified by the Consultant shall not be withheld or delayed by the Owner on account thereof, but the Owner may withhold from the Contract Price until the remaining work is finished only such monies as the Consultant shall determine are sufficient and reasonable to cover the cost of performing such remaining work and adequately to protect the Owner from claims;

project management for Builders and Contractors 143

(b) Where legislation permits and where, upon application by the Contractor, the Consultant has certified that a Subcontract has been totally performed to his/her satisfaction prior to the Substantial Performance of this Contract, the Owner shall pay the Contractor the holdback retained for such Subcontractor on the day following the expiration of the Statutory Limitation Period stipulated in the Mechanics' Lien Act applicable to the place of building.

23.4 Notwithstanding the provisions of 23.3 (b) and notwithstanding the wording of such certificates the Contract shall ensure that such work is protected pending the Total Performance of the Contract and be responsible for the correction of any defects in it regardless of whether or not they were apparent when such certificates were issued.

23.5 The Consultant shall, within ten (10) days of receipt of an application from the Contractor for a certificate of Substantial Performance, make an inspection and assessment of the Work to verify the validity of the application. The Consultant shall within seven (7) days of his/her inspection notify the Contractor of his/her approval or disapproval of the application. When the Consultant finds the Work to be substantially performed he/she shall issue such a certificate. The date of this certificate shall be the date of Substantial Performance of the Contract. Immediately following the issuance of the Certificate of Substantial Performance, the Consultant, in consultation with the Contractor shall establish a reasonable date for the Total Performance of the Contract.

23.6 Following the issue of the Certificate of Substantial Performance and upon receipt from the Contractor of all documentation called for in the Contract Documents and as required by the law of the place of the Work, the Consultant shall issue a certificate for payment of holdback monies. The release of holdback monies authorized by this certificate shall become due and the monies shall be payable on the day following the expiration of the Statutory Limitation Period stipulated in the Mechanics' Lien Act applicable to the place of the Work, or where such legislation does not exist or apply, in accordance with such other legislation, regulations governing privileges, industry practice or such other provisions which may be agreed to between the parties, providing that no lien or privilege claims against the Work exist and the Contractor has submitted to the Owner a sworn statement that all accounts for labour, subcontracts, products, construction machinery and equipment and any other indebtedness which may have been incurred by the Contractor in the Substantial Performance of the Work and for which the Owner might, in any way, be held responsible, have been paid in full except holdback monies properly retained.

23.7 The Consultant shall within ten (10) days of receipt of an application from the Contractor for payment upon Total Performance of the Contract, make an inspection and assessment of the Work to verify the validity of the application. The Consultant shall within seven (7) days of the inspection, notify the Contractor of the approval or disapproval of the application. When the Consultant finds the Work to be totally performed to his/her satisfaction, he/she shall issue a Certificate of the Total Performance and certify for payment the remaining monies due to the Contractor under the Contract less any holdback monies which are required to be retained. The date of this certificate shall be the date of the Total Performance of the Contract. The Owner shall, within five (5) days of issuance of such certificate, make payment to the Contractor in accordance with the provisions of Article A4 of the Agreement.

23.8 The release of any remaining holdback monies shall become due and payable on the day following the expiration of the Statutory Limitation Period stipulated in the Mechanics' Lien Act applicable to the place of building, or where such legislation does not exist or apply in accordance with such other legislation, regulations governing privileges, industry practice or such other provisions which may be agreed to between the parties, provided that no claims against the Work exist and the Contractor has submitted to the Owner a sworn statement that all accounts for labour, subcontracts, products, construction machinery and equipment and any other indebtedness which may have been incurred by the Contractor in the Total

Performance of the Work and for which the Owner might in any way be held responsible have been paid in full except holdback monies properly retained.

23.9 No certificate for payment, or any payment made thereunder, nor any partial or entire use of occupancy of the Work by the Owner shall constitute an acceptance of any work or products not in accordance with the Contract Documents.

23.10 The issuance of the Certificate of Total Performance shall constitute a waiver of all claims by the Owner against the Contractor except those previously made in writing and still unsettled, if any, and those arising from the provisions of GC 33 - Warranty. the acceptance of the Certificate of Total Performance or of the payment due thereunder shall constitute a waiver of all claims by the Contractor against the Owner except those made in writing prior to his/her application for payment upon Total Performance of the Contract and still unsettled, if any.

GC 24   TAXES AND DUTIES

24.1 Unless otherwise stated in Supplementary General Conditions, the Contractor shall pay all government sales taxes, customs duties and excise taxes with respect to the Contract.

24.2 Any increase or decrease in costs to the Contractor, due to changes in such taxes and duties after the date of the Agreement, shall increase or decrease the Contract Price accordingly.

24.3 Where an exemption of government sales taxes, customs duties or excise taxes is applicable to the Contract by way of the Contractor filing claims for, or cooperating fully with the Owner and the proper authorities in seeking to obtain such refunds, the procedure shall be established in a Supplementary General Condition.

GC 25   LAWS, NOTICES, PERMITS AND FEES

25.1 The laws of the place of the Work shall govern the Work.

25.2 The Contractor shall obtain all permits, licences and certificates and pay all fees required for the performance of the Work which are in force at the date of tender submission (but this shall not include the obtaining of permanent easements or rights of servitude).

25.3 The Contractor shall give all required notices and comply with all laws, ordinances, rules, regulations, codes and orders of all authorities having jurisdiction relating to the Work, to the preservation of the public health and construction safety which are, or become in force, during the performance of the Work.

25.4 The Contractor shall not be responsible for verifying that the Contract Documents are in compliance with the applicable laws, ordinances, rules, regulations and codes relating to the Work. If the Contract Documents are at variance therewith, or changes which require modification to the Contract Documents are made to any of the laws, ordinances, rules, regulations and codes by the authorities having jurisdiction subsequent to the date of tender submission, any resulting change in the cost shall constitute a corresponding change in the Contract Price. The Contractor shall notify the Consultant in writing requesting direction immediately any such variance or change is observed by him/her.

25.5 If the Contractor fail to notify the Consultant in writing and obtain his/her direction as required in GC 25.4 and performs any work knowing it to be contrary to any laws, ordinances, rules, regulations, codes and orders of any authority having jurisdiction, he/she shall be responsible for and shall correct any violations thereof and shall bear all costs, expense and damage attributable to his/her failure to comply with the provisions of such laws, ordinances, rules, regulations, codes and orders.

GC 26 PATENT FEES

26.1 The Contractor shall pay all royalties and patent licence fees required for the performance of the Contract. He/she shall hold the Owner harmless from and against all claims, demands, losses, costs, damages, actions, suits or proceedings arising out of the Contractor's performance of the Contract which are attributable to an infringement or an alleged infringement of any patent invention by the Contractor or anyone for whose acts he/she may be liable.

26.2 The Owner shall hold the Contractor harmless against all claims, demands, losses, costs, damages, actions, suits or proceedings arising out of the Contractor's performance of the Contract which are attributable to an infringement of an alleged infringement of any patent or invention in executing anything for the purpose of the Contract, the model, plan or design of which was supplied to the Contractor by the Owner.

GC 27 WORKERS COMPENSATION

27.1 Prior to commencing the Work and prior to receiving payment on Substantial and Total Performance of the Work, the Contractor shall provide evidence of compliance with all requirements of the province or territory of the place of building with respect to worker's compensation including payments due thereunder.

27.2 At any time during the term of Contract, when requested by the Consultant, the Contractor shall provide such evidence of compliance by him/herself and any or all of his/her Subcontractors.

GC 28 LIABILITY INSURANCE

28.1 **Comprehensive General Liability Insurance**

(a) Without restricting the generality of GC 17 - Indemnification, the Contractor shall provide and maintain, either by way of a separate policy or by an endorsement to his/her existing policy, Comprehensive General Liability Insurance acceptable to the Owner and subject to limits of not less than one million dollars inclusive per occurrence for bodily injury, death, and damage to property including loss of use thereof.

(b) The insurance shall be in the joint names of the Contractor, the Owner and the Consultant, and shall also cover as Unnamed Insureds all Subcontractors and anyone employed directly or indirectly by the Contractor or his/her Subcontractors to perform a part or parts of the Work but excluding suppliers whose only function is to supply and/or transport products to the project site.

(c) The insurance shall also include as Unnamed Insureds the architectural and engineering consultants of the Owner and the Consultant.

(d) The insurance shall preclude subrogation claims by the Insurer against anyone insured thereunder.

(e) The Comprehensive General Liability insurance shall include coverage for:

1) premises and operations liability
2) products or completed operations liability
3) blanket contractual liability
4) cross liability
5) elevator and hoist liability
6) contingent employer's liability
7) personal injury liability arising out of false arrest, detention or imprisonment or malicious prosecution; libel, slander or defamation of character;

invasion of privacy, wrongful eviction or wrongful entry.
8) shoring, blasting, excavating, underpinning, demolition, pile driving and caisson work, work below ground surface, tunnelling and grading, as applicable.
9) liability with respect to non-owned licensed vehicles.

28.2 **Automobile liability Insurance**

The Contractor shall provide and maintain liability insurance in respect of owned licensed vehicles subject to limits or not less than one million dollars inclusive.

28.3 **Aircraft and/or Watercraft Liability Insurance**

The Contractor shall provide and maintain liability insurance with respect to owned or non-owned aircraft and watercraft, as may be applicable, subject to limits of not less than one million dollars inclusive. Such insurance shall be in the joint names of the Contractor, the Owner, the Consultant and those parties defined in 28.1 (b) (c) where they have an interest in the use and operation of such aircraft or watercraft. The insurance shall preclude subrogation claims by the Insurer against anyone insured thereunder.

28.4 All liability insurance shall be maintained continuously until twelve (12) months after the date the Consultant issues a certificate of Total Performance.

28.5 The Contractor shall provide the Owner with evidence of all liability insurance prior to the commencement of the Work and shall promptly provide the Owner with a certified true copy of each insurance policy.

28.6 All liability insurance policies shall contain an endorsement to provide all Names Insureds with prior notice of changes and cancellations. Such endorsement shall be in the following form:

"It is understood and agreed that the coverage provided by this policy will not be changed or amended in any way nor cancelled until 30 d days after written notice of such change or cancellation shall have been given to all Named Insureds."

GC 29   PROPERTY INSURANCE

29.1 Except as may be agreed to the contrary and so stipulated in the Supplementary General Conditions (SGC), the Contractor shall provide and maintain property insurance, acceptable to the Owner, insuring the full value of the Work in the amount of the Contract Price and the full value as stated of products that are specified to be provided by the Owner for incorporation in the Work. The insurance shall be in the joint names of the Contractor and the Owner and shall include the interests of the Contractor, the Owner, the Subcontractors and all others having an insurable interest in the Work. The policies shall include all Subcontractors as Unnamed Insureds or, if they specifically request, as Named Insureds. The policies shall preclude subrogation claims by the Insurer against anyone insured thereunder.

29.2 Such coverage shall be provided for by EITHER an All Risks Builders' Risk Policy OR by a combination of a standard Builders' Risk Fire Policy including Extended Coverage and Malicious Damage Endorsements and a Builders' Risk Differences in Conditions Policy providing equivalent coverage.

29.3 The policies shall insure against all risks of direct loss or damage subject to such exclusions as may be indicated in the Supplementary General Conditions (SGC). Such coverage shall apply to:

(a) all products, labour and supplies of any nature whatsoever, the property of the Insureds or of others for which the Insureds may have assumed responsibility, to be used in or pertaining to the site preparations, demolition of existing structures, erection and/or fabrication and/or reconstruction and/or repair of the

project management for Builders and Contractors 147

                insured project, while on the site or in transit, subject to the exclusion of any property specified in the Supplementary General Conditions (SGC);

      (b)   the installation, testing and any subsequent use of machinery and equipment including boilers, pressure vessels or vessels under vacuum;

      (c)   damage to the Work caused by an accident to and/or the explosion of any boiler(s) or pressure vessel(s) forming part of the Work.

                Such coverage shall exclude construction machinery, equipment, temporary structural and other temporary facilities, tools and supplies used in the construction of the Work and which are not expendable under the contract.

29.4   The Contractor shall provide the Owner with evidence of all insurances prior to commencement of the Work and shall promptly provide the Owner with a certified true copy of each insurance policy. Policies shall contain an endorsement to provide all Named Insureds with prior notice of changes and cancellations. Such endorsement shall be in the following form:

"It is understood and agreed that the coverage provided by this policy will not be changed or amended in any way nor cancelled until 30 days after written notice of such change or cancellation shall have been given to all Named Insureds."

29.5   All such insurance shall be maintained continuously until ten (10) days after the date the Consultant issues a certificate of Total Performance. All such insurance shall provide for the Owner to take occupancy of the Work or any part thereof during the term of this insurance. Any increase in the cost of this insurance arising out of such occupancy shall be at the Owner's expense.

29.6   The policies shall provide that, in the event of a loss, payment for damage to the Work shall be made to the Owner and the Contractor as their respective interests may appear. The Contractor shall act on behalf of the Owner and him/herself for the purpose of adjusting the amount of such loss with the Insurers. On the determination of the extent of the loss, the Contractor shall immediately proceed to restore the 'Work and shall be entitled to receive from the Owner (in addition to any sum due under the Contract) the amount at which the Owner's interest in the restoration work has been appraised, such amount to be paid as the work of the restoration proceeds and ion accordance with the Consultant;'s certificates for payment. Damage shall not affect the rights and obligations of either party under the Contract except that the Contractor shall be entitled to such reasonable extension of time for Substantial and Total Performance of the Work as the Consultant may decide.

29.7   The Contractor and his/her Subcontractors as may be applicable shall be responsible for any deductible amounts under the policies and for providing such additional insurance as may be required to protect the Insureds against loss on items excluded from the policies.

GC30   PROTECTION OF WORK AND PROPERTY

30.1   The Contractor shall protect the property adjacent to the Project site from damage as the result of his/her operations under the Contract.

30.2   The Contractor shall protect the Work and the Owner's property from damage and shall be responsible for any damage which may arise as the result of his/her operations under the Contract except damage which occurs as the result of:
      (a)   error in the Contract Documents, and/or
      (b)   acts or omissions by the Owner, his/her agents, employees or Other Contractors.

30.3   Should any damage occur to the Work and/or Owner's property for which the Contractor is responsible he/she shall make good such damage at his/her own expense or pay all costs incurred by others in making good such damage.

30.4 Should any damage occur to the Work and/or Owner's property for which the Contractor is not responsible as provided in GC 30.2 he/she shall make good such damage to the Work and, if the Owner so directs to the Owner's property, and the Contract Price and Contract Time shall be adjusted in accordance with GC 20 - Changes in the Work or the applicable Supplementary General Conditions.

GC 31 DAMAGES AND MUTUAL RESPONSIBILITY

31.1 If either party to this Contract should suffer damage in any manner because of any wrongful act or neglect of the other party or anyone employed by him/her, then he/she shall be reimbursed by the other party for such damage. The party reimbursing the other party shall be subrogated to the rights of the other party in respect of such wrongful act or neglect if it be that of a third party.

31.2 Claims under this GC shall be made in writing to the party liable within reasonable time after the first observance of such damage and not later than the time limits stipulated in GC 23.10 - Certificates and Payments, and may be adjusted by agreement or in the manner set out in GC 16 - Settlement of Disputes.

31.3 If the Contractor has caused damage to any Other Contractor on the Work, the Contractor agrees upon due notice to settle with such Other Contractor by agreement or arbitration, if he/she will so settle. If such Other Contractor sue the Owner on account of any damage alleged to have been so sustained, the Owner shall notify the Contractor and may require the Contractor to defend the action at the Contractor's expense. If any final order or judgment against the Owner arises therefrom, the Contractor shall pay or satisfy it and pay all costs incurred by the Owner.

31.4 If the Contractor becomes liable to pay or satisfy any final order, judgment or award against the Owner then the Contractor, upon undertaking to indemnify the Owner against any and all liability for costs, shall have the right to appeal in the name of the Owner such final order or judgment to any and all courts of competent jurisdiction.

GC 32 BONDS

32.1 The Owner shall have the right during the period stated in the tender documents for acceptance of the tender to require the Contractor to provide and maintain in good standing until the fulfilment of the Contract, bonds covering the faithful performance of the Contract including the requirements of the Warranty provided for in GC 33 - Warranty, and the payment of all obligations arising under the Contract.

32.2 All such bonds shall be issued by a duly incorporated surety company approved by the Owner and authorized to transact a business or suretyship in the Province or Territory of the place of building. The form of such bonds shall be the latest edition of the CCA approved forms.

32.3 If bonds are called for in the tender documents the costs attributable to providing such bonds shall be included in the tender price.

32.4 Should the Owner require the provision of a bond or bonds by the Contractor after the receipt of tenders for the Work, the Contract Price shall be increased by all costs attributable to providing such bonds.

32.5 The Contractor shall promptly provide the Owner, through the Consultant, with any bonds that are required.

GC 33 WARRANTY

33.1 The Contractor shall correct at his own expense any defects in the Work due to faulty products and/or workmanship appearing within a period of one year from the date of Substantial Performance of the Work.

33.2 The Contractor shall correct and/or pay for any damage to other work resulting from any corrections required under the conditions of 33.1.

33.3 Neither the Consultant's final certificate nor payment thereunder shall relieve the

project management for Builders and Contractors

Contractor from his/her responsibility hereunder.
33.4 The Owner and/or Consultant shall give the Contractor written notice of observed defects promptly.
33.5 The Contractor shall be liable for the proper performance of the Work only to the extent that careful workmanship and proper implementation of the Contract Documents will permit and any warranty given respecting the Work and performance shall only be valid so far as the design will permit such performance.
33.6 Nothing in this GC shall be deemed to restrict any liability of the Contractor arising out of any law in force in the Province or Territory.

GC 34 CONTRACTOR'S RESPONSIBILITIES AND CONTROL OF THE WORK

34.1 The Contractor shall have complete control of the Work except as provided in GC 15 - Emergencies. He/she shall effectively direct and supervise the Work using his/her best skill and attention. He/she shall be solely responsible for all construction means, methods, techniques, sequences, and procedures and for coordinating all parts of the Work under the Contract.
34.2 The Contractor shall have the sole responsibility for the design, erection, operation, maintenance and removal of temporary structural and other temporary facilities and the design and execution of construction methods required in their use. The Contractor shall engage and pay for registered professional engineering personnel skilled in the appropriate discipline to perform these functions where required by law or by the Contract Documents and in all cases where such temporary facilities and their method of construction are of such a nature that professional engineering skill is required to produce safe and satisfactory results.
34.3 Notwithstanding the provisions of paragraphs 34.1 and 34.2 above, or any provisions to the contrary elsewhere in the Contract Documents where such Contract Documents include designs for temporary structural and other temporary facilities of specify a method of construction in whole or in part, such facilities and methods shall be deemed to comprise part of the overall design of the Work and the Contractor shall not be held responsible for that part of the design or the specified method of construction. The Contractor shall, however, be responsible for the execution of such design or specified method of construction in the same manner that he/she is responsible for the execution of the Work.
34.4 The Contractor shall carefully examine the Contract Documents and shall promptly report to the Consultant any error, inconsistency or omission he/she may discover. The Contractor shall not be held liable for any damage resulting from any such errors, inconsistencies or omissions in the Contract Documents.

GC 35 SUPERINTENDENCE

35.1 The Contractor shall employ a competent superintendent or delegate superintendence to competent subcontractors as required, who shall be in attendance at the Work site as required for the proper performance of the Work.
35.2 The superintendent shall be satisfactory to the Consultant and shall not be changed except for good reason and only then after consultation with and agreement by the Consultant.
35.3 The superintendent shall represent the Contractor at the Work site and directions given to him/her by the Consultant shall be held to have been given to the Contractor. Important directions shall be confirmed to the Contractor in writing, other directions will be so confirmed if requested.

GC36 LABOUR AND PRODUCTS

36.1 Unless otherwise stipulated elsewhere in the Contract Documents, the Contractor shall provide and pay for all labour, products, tools, construction equipment and machinery, water, heat, light, power, transportation and other facilities and services necessary for the proper performance of the Work.

36.2 All products provided shall be new unless otherwise specified in the Contract Documents. Any products which are not specified shall be of a quality best suited to the purpose required and their use subject to the approval of the Consultant.

36.3 The Contractor shall at all times maintain good order and discipline among his employees engaged on the Work and shall not employ on the Work any unfit person nor anyone not skilled in the task assigned to him/her.

GC37 SUBSURFACE CONDITIONS

37.1 The Contractor shall promptly notify the Consultant in writing if, in his opinion, the subsurface conditions at the site of the Work differ materially from those indicated in the Contract Documents or as may have been represented to him/her by the Owner or Consultant before the time of tender submission.

37.2 After prompt investigation, should the Consultant determine that conditions do differ materially, he/she shall issue appropriate instructions for changes in the Work as provided for in GC20 - Changes in the Work.

GC38 USE OF PREMISES

38.1 The Contractor shall confine his apparatus, the storage of products and the operations of his/her workers to limits indicated by laws, ordinances, permits or by directions of the Consultant and shall not unreasonably encumber the premises with his products.

38.2 The Contractor shall not load or permit to be loaded any part of the Work with a weight that will endanger its safety.

38.3 The Contractor shall enforce the Consultants's instructions regarding signs, advertisements, fires and smoking.

GC39 CLEANUP AND FINAL CLEANING OF WORK

39.1 The Contractor shall maintain the Work in a tidy condition and free from the accumulation of waste products and debris, other than that caused by the Owner, other Contractors or their employees which other waste products or debris shall not be allowed to interfere with the work of this Contractor.

39.2 When the Work is substantially Performed, the Contractor shall remove all his/her surplus products, tools, construction machinery and equipment not required for the performance of the remaining work. The Contractor shall also remove any waste products and debris and leave the Work clean and suitable for occupancy by the Owner unless otherwise specified.

39.3 When the Work is Totally Performed, the Contractor shall remove all of his/her surplus products, tools, construction machinery and equipment . He/she shall also remove any waste products and debris, other than that caused by the Owner, other Contractors or their employees.

GC40 CUTTING AND REMEDIAL WORK

40.1 The Contractor shall do all cutting and remedial work that may be required to make the several parts of the Work come together properly.

40.2 The Contractor shall coordinate the schedule for the Work to ensure that this requirement is kept to a minimum.

40.3 Should the Owner or anyone employed by him/her be responsible for ill-timed work necessitating cutting and/or remedial work to be performed, the cost of such cutting and or remedial work shall be valued as provided in GC21 - Valuation and Certification of Changes in the Work and added to the Contract Price or shall be paid as indicated in the Supplementary General Conditions.

project management for Builders and Contractors 151

40.4 Cutting and remedial work shall be performed by specialists familiar with the materials affected and shall be performed in a manner to neither damage nor endanger and of the Work.

GC41 INSPECTION OF WORK

41.1 The Owner and the Consultant and their authorized representatives shall have access to the Work for inspection wherever it is in preparation or progress. The Contractor shall cooperate to provide reasonable facilities for such access.

41.2 If special tests, inspections or approvals are required by the Contract Documents, the Consultant's instructions or the laws of ordinances of the place of the Work, the Contractor shall give the Consultant timely notice requesting inspection. Inspection by the Consultant shall be made promptly. The Contractor shall arrange inspections by other authorities and shall notify the Consultant of the date and time.

41.3 If the Contractor covers or permits to be covered any of the Work that is subject to inspection or before any special tests and approvals are completed without the approval of the Consultant, the Contractor shall uncover the Work, have the inspections satisfactorily completed and make good the Work at hi/hers own expense.

41.4 The Contractor shall furnish promptly to the Consultant two (2) copies of all certificates and inspection reports relating to the Work.

GC 42 REJECTED WORK

42.1 Defective work, whether the result of poor workmanship, use of defective products or damage through carelessness or other act or omission of the Contractor, and whether incorporated in the Work or not, which has been rejected by the Consultant as failing to conform to the Contract Documents shall be removed promptly from the premises by the Contractor and replaced and/or re-executed promptly in accordance with the Contract Documents at the Contractor's expense.

42.2 Other Contractor's work destroyed or damaged by such removals or replacements shall be made good promptly at the Contractor's expense.

42.3 If in the opinion of the Consultant it is not expedient to correct defective work or work not done in accordance with the Contract Documents, the Owner may deduct from the Contract Price the difference in value between the Work as done and that called for by the Contract, the amount of which shall be determined in the first instance by the Consultant.

GC 43 SHOP DRAWINGS

43.1 The term "shop drawings" means drawings, diagrams, illustrations, schedules, performance charts, brochures and other data which are to be provided by the Contractor to illustrate details of a portion of the Work.

43.2 The Contractor shall arrange for the preparation of clearly identified shop drawings as called for by the Contract Documents or as the Consultant may reasonably request.

43.3 Prior to submission to the Consultant, the Contractor shall review all shop drawings. By this review the Contractor represents that he/she has determined and verified all field measurements, field construction criteria, materials, catalogue numbers and similar data or will do so and that he/she has checked and coordinated each shop drawing with the requirements of the Work and of the Contract Documents. The Contractor's review of each shop drawing shall be indicated by stamp, date and signature of a responsible person.

43.4 The Contractor shall submit shop drawings to the Consultant for this review with reasonable promptness and in orderly sequence so as to cause no delay in the Work or in the Work of Other Contractors. If either the Contractor of the Consultant so requests, they shall jointly prepare a schedule fixing the dates for submission and return of shop drawings. Shop drawings shall be submitted in the form of a reproducible transparency or prints as the Consultant may direct. At the time of submission the Contractor shall notify the Consultant in writing of any deviations in the shop drawings from the requirements of the Contract Documents.

43.5 The Consultant shall review and return shop drawings in accordance with any schedule agreed upon, or otherwise with reasonable promptness so as to cause no delay. The Consultant's review shall be for conformity to the design concept and for general arrangement only and such review shall not relieve the Contractor of responsibility for errors or omissions in the shop drawings or of responsibility for meeting all requirements of the Contract Documents unless a deviation on the shop drawings has been approved in writing by the Consultant.

43.6 The Contractor shall make any changes in shop drawings which the Consultant may require consistent with the Contract Documents and re-submit unless otherwise directed by the Consultant. When re-submitting the Contractor shall notify the Consultant in writing of any revisions other than those requested by the Consultant.

GC 44   SAMPLES

44.1 The Contractor shall submit for the Consultant's approval such standard manufacturers' samples as the Consultant may reasonably require. Samples shall be labelled as to origin and intended use in the Work and shall conform to the requirements of the Contract Documents.

44.2 The Contractor shall submit for the Consultant's approval such standard manufacturers' samples as the Consultant may reasonably require. Samples shall be labelled as to origin and intended use in the Work and shall conform to the requirements of the Contract Documents.

44.3 The Contractor shall provide samples of special products, assemblies, or components when so specified. The cost of such samples not specified shall be authorized as an addition to the Contract Price as provided in GC 20 - Changes in the Work.

GC 45   TESTS AND MIX DESIGNS

45.1 The Contractor shall furnish to the Consultant test results and mix designs as may be requested.

45.2 The cost of tests and mix designs beyond those called for in the Contract Documents or beyond those required by laws, ordinances, rules and regulations relating the Work and the preservation of public health, shall be authorized as an addition to the Contract Price as provided in GC 20 - Changes in the Work or the applicable Supplementary General Conditions.

As an example of Supplementary General Conditions, those that follow were for a contract for which the Owner (Client) wished to perform his own inspection, being unwilling to pay the additional fee to the Designer.

SUPPLEMENTARY GENERAL CONDITIONS

These Supplementary General Conditions are attached to and form part of the Contract Between John and Mary Doe (Owners) and Better Builders Inc. (Contractor) dated x/xx/xx

SGC01 For the purposes of this Contract, the Owner shall be deemed to be the Designer. The Owner by acting for him/herself accepts all the responsibilities invested by the terms of this Contract in the Designer and will perform those functions in a proper and timely manner in order to prevent delays in the prosecution of the Work.

SGC02	In the event of no consultant being employed by the Owner, then interpretation of the Contract Documents shall be by mutual agreement of the Owner and the Contractor. Should they fail to agree on a question of interpretation, then recourse must be made to GC16 - Settlement of Disputes.
SGC03	The Owner shall supply contract documentation, being drawings, specifications, soil reports, etc.
SGC04	GC18 - Contingency Allowance is not applicable
SGC05	GC20 - Changes in the Work and GC21: Changes shall be authorized in writing
SGC06	GC26 - Patent Fees is not applicable
SGC07	GC32 - Bonds is not applicable
SGC08	The Contractor declares that he/she has proper insurance to cover the responsible performance of the Work and that the requirements of GC28 - Liability Insurance have been met
SGC09	The Owner shall supply electricity and water, at no cost to the Contractor, sufficient to perform the work required by the Contract Documents.

STIPULATED PRICE PLUS FEE

The following contract was based on the CCDC format and was for a very large renovation project for which complete specifications could not be written due the many unknowns anticipated as the work progressed. So the Builder agreed to work for a fee plus the cost of time and materials and sub-contract costs. The Agreement part of the contract and the Supplementary General Conditions of the Contract are set out below. The General Conditions were the same as for the Stipulated Price Contract.

AGREEMENT BETWEEN OWNER AND CONTRACTOR

This Agreement made in duplicate this eighth day of August, 2001

by and between John and Jane Doe jointly and severally, hereinafter called the **Owner**, and Better Builders Inc., hereinafter called the **Contractor**,

witnesseth: that the Owner and the Contractor undertake and agree as follows:

A-1 **THE WORK**

The Contractor agrees to:

a) perform all the Work required by the contract documents for renovations to the property known as 3886 Carlington Blvd., Victoria which documents have been initialled by the parties, and which were prepared by Victoria and Victoria Associates, acting as and hereinafter called the Architect and

b) do and fulfil everything indicated by this Agreement, and

c) commence the work within one week of receiving the Contract Documents or sooner at the discretion of the Contractor and, subject only to adjustment as provided for in the Contract Documents, attain Substantial Performance of the Work, as mutually agreed by the Owner and Contractor, within sixty (60) working days of commencement of the Work, except as shall be otherwise agreed in writing between the parties.

A-2 CONTRACT DOCUMENTS

The following is an exact list of the Contract Documents referred to in Article A-1 of this Agreement and as defined in item 2 of DEFINITIONS. This list is subject to subsequent amendments in accordance with the provisions of the Contract and agreed upon between the parties. Terms used in the Contract Documents which are defined in the attached DEFINITIONS shall have the meanings designated in those definitions.

1. this Agreement
2. Definitions
3. General Conditions
4. Supplementary General Conditions
5. Description of the Work.
6. Drawings provided by the Architect as listed below:
7. any subsequently agreed amendments or changes to the Contract

A-3 CONTRACT FEE

In consideration of the performance of the Work, the Owner agrees to pay the Contractor in Canadian funds a contract fee as follows:

1. A percentage fee against all project costs of twenty percent (20%) of the Cost of the Work, earned as the Cost of the Work accrues for overhead and profit

The Contract Fee shall be subject to adjustment as may be required in accordance with the provisions of the Contract Documents. Such adjustments shall be made in respect of additions or deletions to the work duly authorized by the Consultant on behalf of the Owner and shall be subject to the same percentage fees as the Work described in the Description of the Work.

A-4 PAYMENT

(a) Subject to applicable legislation and the provisions of the Contract Documents, and in accordance with legislation and statuary regulations respecting holdback percentages, the Owner shall:
1. make an initial payment to the Contractor of five thousand dollars ($5,000.00) as an advance against the COST OF THE WORK, which amount is to be deducted from the penultimate payment (Substantial Performance of the Work) by the Owner to the Contractor from such costs and fees remaining due, and
2. make bi-weekly payments to the Contractor in Canadian funds on account of the Cost of the Work performed to date and products delivered to the Place of the Work or other locations designated by the Owner, the amount of such payments to be as certified by the Consultant, and
3. make bi-weekly payments to the Contractor in Canadian funds on account of the Contract Fees earned as described in Article A-3 CONTRACT FEE.
4. upon Substantial Performance of the Work as certified by the Consultant pay to the Contractor the unpaid balance of holdback monies when due in accordance with paragraph 14.4 of GC 14 - CERTIFICATES AND PAYMENTS and paragraph A-4 (a)(1) above, and
5. upon Total Performance of the Work as certified by the Consultant pay to the

Contractor the unpaid monies when due in accordance with paragraph 14.4 of GC 14 - CERTIFICATES AND PAYMENTS.

(b) In the event of loss or damage occurring where payment becomes due under the property and boiler insurance policies, payments shall be made to the Contractor in accordance with the provisions of GC 20 - INSURANCE.

(c) If the Owner fail to make payments to the Contractor as they become due under the terms of this Contract or in an award by arbitration or court, interest of two percent (2%) per month, twenty-four percent (26.8%) per annum on such unpaid amounts shall also become due and payable. Such interest shall be calculated from the date of the first default and added to any unpaid amounts on a bi-weekly basis.

A-5 RIGHTS AND REMEDIES

(a) The duties and obligations imposed by the Contract Documents and the rights and remedies available thereunder shall be in addition to and not a limitation of any duties, obligations, rights and remedies otherwise imposed or available by law.

(b) No action or failure to act by the Owner, Consultant or Contractor shall constitute a waiver of any right or duty afforded any of them under the Contract, nor shall any such action or failure to act constitute an approval of or acquiescence in any breach thereunder, except as may be specifically agreed in writing.

A-6 RECEIPTS OF AND ADDRESSES FOR NOTICES

Communications in writing between the parties or between them and the Consultant shall be considered to have been received by the addressee on the date of delivery if delivered by hand to the individual or to a member of the firm or to an officer of the corporation for whom they are intended or, if sent by post or by telegram, to have been delivered within five (5) working days of the date of mailing, dispatch or of delivery to the telegraph company when addressed as follows:

The Owner at:
The Contractor at:
The Consultant at:

A-7 LAW OF THE CONTRACT

The law of the Place of the Work shall govern the interpretation of the Contract.

A-8 LANGUAGE OF THE CONTRACT

At the request of the parties hereto, the language of the Contract shall be English (French etc).

A-9 SUCCESSION

The General Conditions of the Contract hereto annexed, and all the other aforesaid Contract Documents, are to be read into and form part of the Agreement and the whole shall constitute the Contract between the parties and, subject to law and the provisions of the Contract Documents, shall enure to the benefit of and be binding upon the parties hereto, their respective heirs, legal representatives, successors and assigns.

In witness whereof the parties have executed this Agreement under their respective corporate seals and by the hands of their proper officers thereunto duly authorized.

SIGNED, SEALED AND DELIVERED
in the presence of:

Owner   **Contractor**

_____   _____
name   name

_____   _____
signed   signed

_____   _____
name   name

_____   _____
signed   signed

SUPPLEMENTARY GENERAL CONDITIONS

These Supplementary General Conditions are attached to and form part of the Contract Between .... and .... dated .... ,1994

SGC01	For the purposes of this Contract, the Owner shall be deemed to be the Consultant. The Owner by acting for him/herself accepts all the responsibilities invested by the terms of this Contract in the Consultant and will perform those functions in a timely manner in order to prevent delays in the prosecution of the Work.
SGC02	In the event of there being no consultant employed by the Owner then interpretation of the Contract Documents shall be by mutual agreement of the Owner and the Contractor. Should they fail to agree on a question of interpretation, then recourse must be made to GC16 - Settlement of Disputes.
SGC03	The Contractor shall supply contract documentation, being drawings, specs
SGC04	GC18 - Contingency Allowance is not applicable
SGC05	GC19 not applicable
SGC06	GC20 - Changes in the Work and GC21 shall not apply in respect of valuation of a change. Changes shall be authorized in writing but shall be paid for on the basis of cost plus those percentages of cost previously agreed by the Parties.
SGC07	GC25 - Laws, Notices, Permits and Fees. The Owner shall reimburse the Contractor for all fees required for the performance of the Work and they shall be subject to the same percentages of cost previously agreed by the Parties.
SGC08	GC26 - Patent Fees is not applicable
SGC09	GC32 - Bonds is not applicable
SGC10	The Contractor declares that he/she has proper insurance to cover the responsible performance of the Work and that the requirements of GC28 - Liability Insurance

SGC11   The Owner shall supply electricity and water, at no cost to the Contractor, sufficient to perform the work required by the Contract Documents

ANNEX "A"

Description of the Work

The Work consists of the supply of all labour, materials, equipment and supervision to perform the work as described below:: *a description of the work (scope) would follow ...*

PROPOSAL AS A CONTRACT

At the beginning of Section (4), it is recommended that a simple proposal may be used as a form of contract for a small project. This is not completely satisfactory but preferable to no description of the work and no contract. It is still preferable to use the "stipulated price" contract format set out above. The following is an example of a typical proposal to be used as a form of Agreement when "accepted" by the Client.

BETTER BUILDERS INC.   XXX, SATISFIED BLVD.,Victoria, B.C., X2X 1X1
Tel: (604) 000-0000
Fax: (604) 000-0000

PROPOSAL

To	:	Smith Family
Location	:	3836 Cardogan Road, Victoria, B.C.
Date	:	April 26, 2000
Project Title	:	**Bathroom Renovation**
Scope of Work	:	Supply labour, materials and supervision as required at the site of the work to perform the work described below in accordance with all applicable codes and to the requirements of Authorities having jurisdiction:

A GENERAL PRELIMINARY
1. Inspect premises with Client to clarify Scope of Work
2. Protect areas adjacent to the site of the work
3. Remove all cabinets & counter-tops after plumbing disconnections
4. Remove existing tile floor
5. Install sub-floor and/or underlayment as required (sub-floor glued & nailed with barbed or glue-dipped nails at 5 degree angle)

B PLUMBING & MECHANICAL
1. Disconnect and remove all existing plumbing fixtures
2. Install & connect the following fixtures:
   - a)   1 Crane Radcliffe WC with #5 seat
   - b)   1 Crane Coronet basin
   - c)   1 Teck lever handle basin faucet
   - d)   1 Crane porcelain enamelled steel tub
3. Install 1 mirror, 36" x 36", bevel-edged 1/4" plate glass

4 Towel bars to a total length of 7' 6" fitted as agreed with Client
5 Recessed paper holder
6 Recessed, mirrored medicine cabinet
7 Exhaust fan (100 cfm) **(Lump Sum Allowance $350)**

C ELECTRICAL
1 Dismantle & remove existing light fixtures
2 Install one (1) 4ft double tube fluor. fixture
3 Electrical connections & switch for exhaust fan

cntd ....
D TILES
1 Install ceramic tile floor & baseboard to Client's choice **(Lump Sum Allowance $1,200)**

E PAINTING
1 Prime as required & paint 2 topcoats throughout Gliddens Lifemaster 2000 Latex

F GENERAL
1 Clean up & remove all debris to dump for environmentally correct disposal

Total Contract Amount including all lump-sum allowances: **$ 6,125.00**
GSTax @ 7% $ 428.75
TOTAL   **$ 6,553.75**

SCHEDULE OF PAYMENTS
10% On signing contract   10% Commencement of work
25% Completion of demolition   25% Completion of plumbing & electrical
20% Substantial Completion   10% Hold-back on all payments, due 41 days after substantial completion

The work shall be performed in accordance with the National Building Code, CMHC requirements and the regulations of Authorities having jurisdiction over the Work and the site of the Work. This proposal is calculated on the basis of current material and labour costs and is valid for a period of 60 days. Additions and deletions to the Scope of the Work are to be confirmed previously in writing by both parties at an agreed cost or to be charged at cost plus 20% failing agreement between the parties. Late payments will result in stoppage of work until payment is received or agreement reached in respect of the late payment. Payments in arrears of more than 30 days will bear interest charges of 2% per month or 26.8% per annum. Choice of materials not specified or otherwise previously agreed between the Client and the Contractor shall be at the discretion of the Contractor and to standards normally acceptable in the building industry for the type of work covered by this agreement.

Respectfully submitted by: Norman Austin
                                    BETTER BUILDERS INC.

ACCEPTANCE: You are hereby authorized to perform the work as described in this proposal for which the undersigned agrees to pay the sum quoted according to the terms stipulated.

Signed _____ Date _____

SOME NOTES TO THE READER

- This is the document that **could** be used as a substitute for proper plans and specifications. It becomes the Scope of Work once it has been accepted by the Client. It does not, in fact, replace a proper contract but, considering the low value of the work described ($6,125.00), I am prepared to wager that it is much, much better than the Agreement presently used by most small contractors. Your average Client will understand that he/she has made a contractual commitment and will appreciate that he/she is not entitled to expect anything beyond the work you have described.
- In the final paragraph that begins "The work shall be performed in accordance with the ...." the Builder should insert the appropriate standards. The mention of CMHC for Canadian builders is to provide a standard that meets normal use requirements but does not allow for luxury finishes. For instance a third top-coat of paint would have to be mentioned specifically in the Scope of Work. Quality standards are difficult to define in any contract documents but, by (in this case) quoting CMHC, you have made it pretty clear that this work, while being of good quality, does not include marble fixtures or other luxuries. For instance, the light fixture is not described in detail. The Builder need only provide what is usual in this type of work in the area in which the Builder works.
- It is possible that a Client reading the fine print in the last paragraph may object to a mark-up of 20%. There is no reason to do so as this only becomes valid if the Client and Contractor fail to agree on a price for additional work. The Builder is always in a position to say "If you do not agree the price, I am quite happy **not** to do the extra work".

> There was a Builder in Jamaica who refused to make any changes or perform any extra work on a project until after Substantial Completion (Substantial Performance). He maintained that he always finished to schedule and most clients changed their minds about wanting extra work or changes made when they were ready to take occupancy!

- In respect of that 20% mark-up, the Client may ask what is "cost". This is debatable. I see the 20% mark-up on cost as representing profit and "inconvenience" such as inability to proceed with other projects and so on. In other words, I would add it to cost of materials, labour, overheads and supervision. After all, if the Client does not know what he or she wants, it cannot be expected that the Builder will stand around waiting for the **possibility** of extra work or changes. You may be asked to prove your "cost" by the submission of invoices and time-sheets. This is quite justified and is common practice for all costs on "cost-plus" work; it also gives the Builder another reason for being meticulous in the maintenance of records and receipts.

♦ There is a disclaimer at the beginning of this book. Read it and think about it. I am not a lawyer, though I have written a good many contracts. No Builder should be operating without periodic reference to a lawyer about the validity of his/her contractual procedures. If you mean to stay out of trouble, if you are sincere in wanting to do a good job, **see a lawyer** before you start business or as soon as you can if you are already in business and have not done so.

CHANGE ORDER

For whatever reason it is issued, the Change Order (CO) is a legal document and it alters the content of the contract. It **usually** changes the price of the work (increase or decrease) and it often changes the completion date. For this reason, it is important to justify the change fully. The description of the work described in the change should be **complete.**

On large contracts with an Architect or other consultant representing the Client, the problem is sometimes lessened because the Architect issues the CO and describes the work involved.

However (and it is a big 'however"), they often do not do a thorough job. Some architects give a bare-bones description, expecting the Builder to provide a proper description that the Architect can then edit or rationalize. The Builder is going to estimate the work and quote a price. It is for the Architect to make the work and its value seem as little as possible and for the Builder to make it seem extraordinarily complex and time-consuming and, of course, costly. The small Builder may have to write the CO him/herself as the Client most probably will not have the knowledge to do so.

So, big or small, it is important to the Builder to develop the art of writing a Change Order. The important thing, as I said above, is to make it seem like a major undertaking. There are two reasons for this:

♦ it makes the Builder concentrate on what is involved in the work, what materials and labour are required and how it may affect other work considering all the impacts makes an accurate estimate more probable;
♦ the Client is much more likely to approve the work if it is properly described in such detail as makes the price seem reasonable - *one small problem with this is that the Client may decide the work is too complex and refuse to make the change; this is not always a problem, as changes are usually an enormous inconvenience to the Builder, anyway.*

An example: the Builder is providing an addition to a house and the Client decides, when the work is near complete, to change the counter-tops in the existing kitchen, not previously involved in the work. His instruction to the Builder may be as simple as: *"Please quote me for changing the counter-tops in the kitchen".*

project management for Builders and Contractors

The Builder has a couple or more of choices. The addition is nearly complete and there may be another project to be started elsewhere; the Builder may not be really interested in the work but willing to accept it if the price is a good one. In this circumstance, he or she writes in the Change Order:

Supply materials, labour, and supervision to replace counter-tops in the existing kitchen. Protect adjacent surfaces and repair as required.

Cost of the work	*$ 1,250.00*
Taxes	*$ 00.00*
Total	*$ 1,250.00*

Extension of Contract Time maximum 8 working days

On the other hand, the Builder may be really interested in doing the work, though not prepared to make other than an acceptable profit. So the CO could read:

1. *Inspect the location of the proposed counter-top replacement;*
2. *Verify that walls are at 90 degrees to each other;*
3. *Check existing plumbing to ascertain costs of temporary disconnections and re-connections and the need for new plumbing fittings or fixtures;*
4. *Protect existing floor surfaces with 1/4" hardboard or similar, cutting to size to minimize damage;*
5. *Remove major appliances from kitchen to temporary storage area indicated by Client;*
6. *Disconnect plumbing fittings and fixtures;*
7. *Detach existing counter-top from base cabinets, avoiding damage as much as possible to cabinets and existing walls;*
8. *Supply and install new melamine-finished, roll-form counter-top, carefully mitring corners to suit existing walls;*
9. *Re-connect and/or replace plumbing fixtures and fittings; allow for replacement of some fittings;*
10. *Protect finished surface of new counter-top;*
11. *Make good any damage to surfaces adjacent to new counter-top;*
12. *Replace major appliances and remove protective floor covering;*
13. *Clean-up and remove debris from site;*

Sub-Total	*$ 625.00*
Supervision	*$ 120.00*
Overhead at 26%	*$ 194.00*
Profit at 5%	*$ 47.00*
TOTAL	***$ 986.00***
Taxes	*$ 000.00*
GRAND TOTAL	***$ 986.00***

Extension of Contract Time maximum 5 working days
cntd.........

Notes:
1. *Client to select counter-top colour and type within three working days of authorization of this change from a selection provided by the Builder.*
2. *Client is responsible for emptying all cabinet cupboards and drawers and removing appliances and other articles from counter-top to location outside kitchen.*

The first, brief method of describing the work leaves the Builder open to the danger of disagreement with the Client on the detail of the work to be done in the same way that a skimpy Proposal or Scope of Work do. This brevity may cause some disagreement when the work is finished as to exactly what was supposed to have been done. For which reason, I **always** prefer the second example.

There is very little to argue with there. You may consider that it does not cover every detail and you may be right: but there is not **much** left to the imagination. It can be made more convincing by putting a price or an allowance against each line item. This gives the Client the opportunity to say that he/she will forgo that item. The Client, could, for instance, decide personally to move the major appliances or to omit the floor protection (perhaps the existing floor is scheduled for replacement later). And so on. If there is a requirement for a new plumbing fixture (a sink, for example), its cost and its installation would be additional to the price quoted - because it is not included in the description.

CHANGE ORDER FORMAT

There are a great many ways that the information may be presented. Each Architect or Engineer will have his/her own method. If you, the Builder, are required to submit a Change Order because the Client cannot, then the form below may be suitable

.BETTER BUILDERS INC.   XXX, SATISFIED BLVD.,Victoria, B.C., X2X 1X1
Tel: (604) 000-0000
Fax: (604) 000-0000

CHANGE ORDER

C.O. Number: _____   Date: _____

OWNER/CLIENT:

CONSULTANT :

PROJECT   TITLE: _____
PROJECT NO:_____

project management for Builders and Contractors

Under the terms of the Contract it is required that the Contractor perform the work described below.
Description of the work:

*here describe in **detail***

Original Contract Price $
Value of Changes to Date $
Value of this Change $

Revised Contract Price $

Site Instruction Reference: _____

Agreed extension of Contract Time:_____ days / weeks to Total contract time of _____

Authorized by: _____
Name/Title: _____

RECEIVED BY: _____ Date: _____ Time: _____
Better Builders Inc.

ADMINISTRATIVE COST OF A CHANGE ORDER

In theory there is no reason why you should not charge an administration fee for all changes. This may not be agreeable to all your Clients and, for that reason, it should be stated in a clause in the Supplementary General Conditions of the Contract as, for instance:

"All changes or proposed changes to the Contract initiated by the Client or the Client's authorized representative shall be subject to an administrative charge of $50.00, additional to the cost of the work, whether or not the work be performed and whether or not the Price of the Work be increased or decreased thereby or should there be no change in the Price of the Work. This fee shall be added to the cost of the Work and be reimbursed as work progresses."

This has the healthy effect of giving a reason for second thoughts on the part of the Client who might indulge in whimsical proposals for Changes that cost the Builder substantial administrative time. Stipulate the amount of the "fee" per Change in accordance with what you know or anticipate about the Client.

SITE INSTRUCTION

Never accept an oral instruction that is not backed up by a written one. There are three major reasons for the issuance of a Site Instruction:

- The Architect or an inspector with jurisdiction over the work perceives an emergency, gives an oral instruction and then backs it up with a written one (a Site Instruction). Both of these bodies should have a proper form for the Instruction.
- The Client or the Client's Representative perceives the need for something that is not contained in the contract documents; or perhaps the Builder believes the "something" is not in the contract documents and there is the probability of a dispute about the matter. In this case the Client or Rep. may issue a written instruction to perform the work with a note that a price for the work will be negotiated if it is determined that it is not part of the contract.
- The Builder concludes that there is a requirement for additional work to permit the proper performance of the contract. In this case, the Builder requests a written instruction from the Client or Rep.

You may think of many other conditions where an instruction may be given to do something that is not part of the contract. Obviously the Change Order is the proper mechanism for a change in the content of the contract and this may be noted on the Site Instruction. However, this particular form is to take care of those things that need to be done but which cannot be finalized in scope or price or schedule immediately. It is something of an emergency document. Because the Client may not have such a form available, the Builder should always have a few copies on hand.

All instructions must be in writing

The form that follows will suit most situations.

BETTER BUILDERS INC. XXX, SATISFIED BLVD., Victoria, B.C., X2X 1X1
Tel: (604) 000-0000
Fax: (604) 000-0000

SITE INSTRUCTION

S.I.Number: _____   Date: _____
OWNER/CLIENT:
CONSULTANT :
PROJECT TITLE:
PROJECT NUMBER:

Under the terms of the Contract between **Better Builders Inc**. and _____
_____ it is required that the Contractor perform the work described below.

Description of the work:

Change Order Reference: _____ (if applicable)
Anticipated extension of Contract Time:_____ days / weeks

Authorized by: _____
Name/Title: _____

The above work may he subject of a **Change Order** to be issued and authorized by the appropriate authority (Consultant or Owner/Client); except in the case of a "cost-plus" contract in which instance the work shall be reimbursed on the basis of time and material plus the agreed fees.
RECEIVED BY:_____ Date: _____ Time: _____

PURCHASE ORDER

This document (for want of a complete CCDC type of contract) will give you a better control of the activities of your Sub-contractors than a form torn out of a duplicate book bought at your local stationer.

BETTER BUILDERS INC.   XXX, SATISFIED BLVD.,Victoria, B.C., X2X 1X1
Tel: (604) 000-0000
Fax: (604) 000-0000

PURCHASE ORDER (No:)

To   :
Company   :
Address   :

Date   :
Project Title :

Supply the following in accordance with the terms described:

(here a description of the work)

Purchase Price $
GST @ 7% $

TOTAL $

SCHEDULE OF PAYMENTS
____% With Purchase Order
____% Completion of (describe the stage)
____% Completion of (describe the stage)
____% At Substantial Performance (Completion)
____% 41 days after Completion of all work

SCHEDULE OF COMPLETION
The work shall commence no later than _____
The Work shall be completed by _____ *see next page*

OTHER TERMS
All construction work shall be to the minimum standards of the National Building Code, the British Columbia Building Code, the Standards of the Central Mortgage and Housing Corporation, applicable codes of Authorities having jurisdiction over the Work, the requirements of material manufacturers and suppliers. Safety requirements will be rigorously enforced. Any fines, penalties or other charges levied against Better Builders Inc. due to failure on the part of this Supplier to comply with rules, regulations and instructions of "Authorities Having Jurisdiction" will be deducted from payment due to the Supplier. Any change in the work and the cost to be charged therefor shall be previously authorized in writing. This Purchase Order is issued on the basis of current material and labour costs and is valid for a period of 120 days. Additions & deletions to the Scope of the Purchase Order shall be agreed in writing by both parties both as to scope and price. Failure to comply with the terms of this Purchase Order may result in stoppage of the work until compliance is achieved or agreement reached in respect of the continuation of the work. Continued failure to comply with the terms of this Purchase Order may result in Better Builders Inc., making other arrangements for completion of the Work. Choice of materials not specified or otherwise previously agreed between the Client and the Contractor shall be to minimum current standards normally acceptable in the building industry for the type of work covered by this agreement. This Supplier has seen and agrees to accept the General Conditions of the Contract between the Client and Better Builders Inc., as applying equally to the Work included in this Purchase Order.

Purchase Order issued by: _____
An authorized official of:
Better Builders Inc.

ACCEPTANCE: I agree to perform the work described in this Purchase Order according to the terms stipulated.

_____ Date:

_____
signed

PLAN OF OPERATION

The Plan of Operation (POP) and the importance of giving as much consideration as possible, as time will permit and as you become gradually convinced of its usefulness, has been mentioned previously. Here is an outline of a simple POP that will provide most of the information that you need to perform a small project - up to and including a one-off house construction.

BETTER BUILDERS INC.   XXX, SATISFIED BLVD.,Victoria, B.C., X2X 1X1
POP Prepared by: ....
Project Name: **House Construction at: 3866 Carlington Blvd.**
Project Number: ....
Date of POP: ....   Revised Date: .... By: ....

PLAN OF OPERATION

Contents

1	*LFA - Logical Framework Analysis* (for those who find it useful)		
2	**WBS - Work Breakdown Structure**		
3	**Budget and Cash-flow**		
4	**Organigram (Organization Chart)**		
5	**Execution Schedule**		
6	**Payment Plan**		
7	**Contracts**		
7.1	Client		
7.1.1	Standard form of Stipulated Price with (Client's Name)		
7.2	Sub-contractors		
7.2.1	Purchase Orders		
7.2.1	a) Foundations AA Excavation		
	b) Framing BB Carpentry		
	c) Roofing Roofers Inc.		
	d) Etcetera		
8	**Evaluation Milestones**		
8.1	Closing in	Start Date:	Finish Date:
8.2	Drywall Installation	Start Date:	Finish Date:
8.3	Cabinetry & Finish Carpentry	Start Date:	Finish Date:
8.4	Painting	Start Date:	Finish Date:
8.5	External Works	Start Date:	Finish Date:
8.6	Substantial Completion	Start Date:	Finish Date:
8.7	Final Completion	Start Date:	Finish Date:
8.8	End of Warranty Period	Start Date:	Finish Date:
9	**Evaluation Criteria** *(use these to compare actual value at each milestone and at completion against projected cost)*		
9.1	Quality of finish		
9.2	Percentage completion		
9.2	Likelihood of warranty work		
9.3	*etc. etc. etc.*		

This POP format should be adequate for an even larger construction. The variable is the amount of detail included. On a large project, it is likely that there would be a greater variety of contract formats. Some Sub-contractors may be working on a cost-plus basis, some a stipulated sum and so on. For item 3, "Budget & Cash-flow" a reference to a computer file might be sufficient if there is more information than is usefully included in a printed document. The same may apply to the Work Breakdown Structure.

APPENDIX 1

Logical Framework Analysis

As a planning and monitoring tool the LFA is unequalled in its simplicity. Its principal virtue is its clear exposition and arrangement of data. Being in the form of a chart on one sheet of paper, it lends itself to instant appraisal; the logic of the relationships between elements is apparent and it contains the fundamental evaluation criteria. For those not fully familiar with the method, an outline explanation follows.

Goal, Purpose, Outputs and Inputs are described in the "Planning" section but, briefly, they are defined as follows:

Goal   The objective of the program of which the project is a part; the long-term or overall objective.
Purpose   What the project should achieve; what the completion of the Outputs generates.
Outputs   The end results (usually physical) of the management of the Inputs.
Inputs   Resources of time, material, activities which, properly managed, produce the Outputs.

The traditional arrangement of the columns within the table is shown below.

	NARRATIVE SUMMARY	OBJECTIVELY VERIFIABLE INDICATORS	MEANS OF VERIFICATION	IMPORTANT (CRITICAL) ASSUMPTIONS
Goal				
Purpose				
Outputs				
Inputs				

The Project Manager (PM) is immediately responsible for the first two levels of the vertical logic of the approach (inputs & outputs). The PM defines the Inputs that will provide the Outputs and is directly accountable for their control. In most organizations, a higher level of control (the Client - who may be a superior within your organization) decides that the Outputs will produce the Purpose within the context of the Goal. The small builder will decide all the levels.

The vertical logic of the chart indicates the relationships between Input, Output, Purpose and Goal. If the right Inputs are provided and properly managed, then the Outputs will inevitably be produced; the same applies to the subsequent two levels. **Except** that another inevitability is the tendency for things to go wrong. There are bound to be uncertainties - weather, strikes, soaring lending rates, shortage of competent personnel - all the things one cannot know with absolute assurance.

So, at every level, these uncertainties have to be considered and accounted for to the best of one's capacity in the context of experience and the information available at the time. Defining these uncertainties in the column "Important Assumptions" does two things. In the planning stage it conditions the results of the Narrative Summary column at the next higher level in the chart. During implementation it provides a warning that there are possible adverse circumstances of which the PM and the Team must be constantly aware and against which provision must be made.

For instance, a construction project that is to commence under winter conditions might be substantially delayed by excessive frost. In such a case, it would be essential that this be considered and shown under "Important Assumptions". At a higher level, if the building is to be an example of the quality of your work and your Subs have failed to provide the finishes you expected, the Purpose (let us say, "establish reputation for quality") might be unachievable for obvious reasons. In this case the Important Assumption at Output level is that "the Sub-contractors maintain anticipated standards". This Important Assumption in the LFA is a constant reminder of the need to maintain adequate supervision in order to ensure that you and the Client get the quality that you are looking for.

If the Output is not achieved to schedule and the Purpose is consequently foregone, so the achievability of the Goal will be jeopardized.

The two essential columns that define the logic of the approach are "Narrative Summary" and "Important Assumptions". These must be correct (as far as possible) at each level in order to validate the Narrative Summary at the next level.

However, "Objectively Verifiable Indicators" (OVI) are indispensable to rational judgement, indicating the type and magnitude of the things that enable you to measure the correctness of your project development criteria. The column "Means of Verification" speaks for itself: these are your sources of information.

OVI permit you to break down the project into components of the magnitude that suits your convenience during the planning stage: they may be expanded or further broken down in your plan of operation or other planning documents. In the format of the LFA, it is easy to add to the listing as new elements are introduced and as new Important Assumptions force themselves on the attention. A hypothetical project is shown below: it is for the construction of a 200 square metre house on a lot to be provided by the Client.

An example of how apparently minor hurdles can prove costly. If you are negotiating to build the house on a lot that the Client is in process of purchasing, all your time spent estimating, planning and negotiating may be wasted if legal counsel advises that the title to the land is clouded and that the Client should not complete the purchase. Obviously, you would not build until the title was clear but overheads are a significant building cost and time wasted is profits jeopardized. If the house is on a lot or plot in a tract development, title problems are unlikely to arise; the title to the land may not be an "Important Assumption". If it is rural land, there may be problems associated with environment, zoning regulations, etc. In such a case the risk is greater and should be considered in your planning - in your LFA.

NARRATIVE SUMMARY	OBJECTIVELY VERIFIABLE INDICATORS	MEANS OF VERIFICATION	IMPORTANT ASSUMPTIONS
GOAL achieve 5% return on annual $5 million turnover in 10 years	profits increasing annually to final 5%	• accountant's audit	• regular flow of projects under effective management • favourable economic environment
PURPOSE establish reputation for quality at reasonable cost	1 architect's approval at *first* inspection 2 complete construction within budget	• architect's final certificate • final payment by client & project accounts	1 Subs perform to required standards 2 no cost overruns
OUTPUTS 1 residential unit 2 site-works	1 200 sq.m. house 2 landscaped lot	• certificate of occupancy	• project plan & schedule achieved
INPUTS 1 interim financing 2 project management 3 sub-trade contractors 4 building site by client 5 executed construction contract	1 $10,000 overdraft 2 3% of project cost 3 $190,000 total 4 title search by lawyer 5 $200,000 value 6 2% profit	1 letter from bank 2 project accounts 3 purchase orders issued 4 lawyer statement 5 PM/client agreement 6 project accounts	1 continuation of overdraft 2 PM committed to project to completion 3 suitable Subs available 4 lawyer was right 5 no adverse acts of God 6 time & quality parameters met

Note: the previous chart has been compressed into 4 columns to increase space available for information.

RESULTS

Logic permits a further step in the planning and analysis of projects. The provision of the Outputs consequent on certain activities applied to the inputs (or inherent in the provision of the inputs) gives certain definable *results* which are more susceptible of interpretation than simple Outputs and Purpose; perhaps a certain amount of subjectivity is required to develop the correct interpretation. This is discussed in some detail in my book *"incredibly easy project management"* for any reader who wishes to consider the LFA in more detail.

APPENDIX 2

Work Breakdown Structure

The example of a Work Breakdown Structure (WBS) that follows is for a typical Canadian residence and is based on the premise of sub-contracting the work by trades. "Drywall", for example, is gypsum wall board (GWB) and includes application and fixing by screw or nail, taping, filling and sanding and usually presumes the previous installation of insulation and vapour barrier. All trades may not have been included but it is of no consequence to the sequence of the breakdown shown in the chart.

Note that "Services" is one sub-contract, broken down at the next level into "Plumbing" and "Electrical". The assumption in this WBS is that you have selected your services contractor as one who does both mechanical and electrical work. You may ask that Sub-contractor to split the work into the two main trades and even ask for a further sub-division as, for instance, "rough and finish", "heating", and "light fixtures" all being included in the "electrical " trade or activity. Now you have the opportunity to make changes, or the Client has that opportunity, to any of the three electrical sub-activities in the full knowledge of how that change would affect the total stipulated price of the contract.

If the Client decides to use gas heating, the electrical heating is shown at level 4 as an isolated amount and can be eliminated from the electrical contract. Because you have selected a contractor that does a total mechanical and electrical service, you can request a new price for a gas installation and incorporate it into the WBS, affecting only the cost of "services" at level 2 and, of course, the total stipulated price of "House" at level 1. Alternatively, you may call another sub-trade to tender for the gas heating.

The detail for the activity (sub-trade) "Paint" is typical for all the sub-trade contracts. In this case, a contingency of 8% has been applied to the cost. This is because, although you know that your contractor is prompt, an excellent worker, that he always keeps to schedule and returns for touching up, nevertheless, he tends to be untidy and you have increased costs for clean-up. Were it an unknown painter, you might have to increase the contingency to 12% or 15% because a painter can make or break a project and you may have to follow a poor performer with your own touch-up or painting crew for which you need extra money. Theoretically, you may back-charge a sub-trade for sloppy work. A tough and well-organized project manager will have smaller contingencies than most.

Of course, you will not draw a WBS with little boxes such as the one for "Paint". If you are using a computer spread sheet or other program, all that information will be fed into the machine. Again, you may simply put all the data onto individual estimating sheets and refer to the sheets on your WBS diagram. If you have a good imagination, you may not need the diagram. However, I am sure that, in most cases you will find that it simplifies your work enormously. The important thing is to appreciate the logic of the breakdown and to use it in conjunction with estimating, organization, interfacing, scheduling and contracting.

WORK BREAKDOWN STRUCTURE

- HOUSE
  - business overhead
  - project management
    - planning
    - estimating
    - supervision
  - site works
    - clear site
    - excavate to grades
    - excavate to foundations
  - foundations
  - framing
  - drywall
  - roof
  - services
    - plumbing
      - fixtures
      - rough & finish
    - electrical
      - rough & finish
      - heating
      - light fixtures
    - drain tile
    - wall tiles
    - cabinetry
    - paint
  - finishes
    - floor covers
      - carpet
        - family room
        - general
      - sheet vinyl
      - marble tile

DETAIL FOR ACTIVITY "PAINT"

20002	PAINT
Cost	$4,000
Contingency	8 %
Total Cost	$ 4,320

INDEX

Accounts
    system 72
Administration
    of contracts 89, 129
    of Packages 84
Agreement 33, 131, 153
    contract 92
    legal 19
Approvals 21, 87
    Client's 88
    harassment of "approver" 87
    in a bureaucracy 75
    sub-contractor 89
Architect 121, 125, 160, 164
    & change order 160
As-built 36, 87
    control & cost 64
    drawings 120
Attitude 13, 14, 21, 47
    of Supervisor 90
    of the Project Manager 15
Back-charge 21, 45, 122
    related to schedule & LFA 119
Bar chart - see Gantt chart
Budget 41, 72, 86
    & WBS 81
    Builder's 41
    evaluation of 127
Builder
    as Client 42
    as Consultant 54, 105
Business plan 29, 38
Business Promotion
    definition 26
Cash-flow 50
CCDC
    contract 130
Certificate
    see Final Certificate 119
Change Order 22, 87, 89, 97, 98, 101, 123, 141, 158-160
    admin. cost of 163
    cost of 141
    detailed 161
    format 162
    in construction management 98
    related to schedule & LFA 119
    request for 99
Chart, Bar - See Gantt Chart
Checking 65, 111
Claims 65
Clerk of Works 22, 103, 111
Client 12, 24, 164
    & Builder relations 122
    & programs 113
    attitude toward 13
    CMHC 159
    contract 92
    referral 26
Commissioning 118
Communication 15, 19, 21, 127
    cost of 67

Completion 21, 36
    project 118
Computer 81, 112
    & packages 85
    & WBS 81, 85
Conflict
    & Construction Management 103
Construction 56
Construction Management 22, 99, 106, 107, 119
    & Conflict within 103
    & cost 106
    & the Small Builder 105
    as a profession 99
    fees 102
    why & why not 100
Consultant 67, 69, 107, 121
    & Client contract 45
    dealing with 125
    Decisions 136
    inspection 117
Contingency 66, 67, 69, 140
    Builder's 69
    Client's 71
    percentages 70
Contract 91
    for Builder/General Contractor 109
    & lawyer 54
    & WBS 83
    CCDC 51, 130
    Client's 129
    cost plus 96
    do not trim 93
    evaluation of 128
    for Construction Manager 108
    for renovation/addition 130
    for small contractor 93
    format 94
    general conditions 134
    grandparent clause 53
    labour-only 89
    legal 91, 130, 159
    legal format 61
    leverage 47
    lump-sum 130
    price 92, 131
    proposal as 157
    splitting 44
    stipulated price 95, 130
    stipulated price + fee 153
    sub-contractor 94
    Time & Material 97
    types 95
    with Client 34 45
    with Sub-contractor 34
Contract Documents
    & lawyer 53
    addenda 52
    see Documentation 41
Contract Package - see "Package"
Contracting
    of Packages 85

Contractor
    sub-contractor relations 46
Control 11, 22, 34, 47, 126
    & communication lines 45
    criteria 126
    of trades 45
    planning of 34, 126
    site 85
Control of money equals control of project 34
Coordination 19, 21, 35, 67, 112
    of trades 48, 49
    site meeting 88
Cost of the Work 62, 105
    & project location 32
Critical path 51
Deficiencies 36, 120
    in Construction Management 122
    sub-contractor 121
    valuation 121
Delay 37, 103, 107, 116, 118, 136
Design
    & quality assurance 110
    good & bad 65
    problems 110
Design/Build 87, 119
    contingency 71
Developer 42, 86
    & WBS 79
Diary 19, 20
    of Supervisor 91
Documentation 20, 41, 51, 66, 70, 92, 129, 131, 153
    drawings & specs. 55
    good & bad 71
    interpretation 65
    review 116
Employees 94
Equipment
    testing 36, 118
Error
    immunity to 115
    responsibility for 116
Estimating 54, 62
    & WBS 67
    and Organigram 67
    confirmation of 75
    methods 66
    overhead 67
Evaluation 19, 37, 127
    strategic 38
    targets 38
Exclusions 60
    of trades 61
Execution (project) 19, 35, 112
    & WBS 75
Extras
    claiming 53
Fees
    & Construction Management 102
Final Certificate
    preparation 119
Financing 38
Follow-up 35, 123, 124
    as an irritant 124 ...cntd.
    in writing 37, 123
    of inaction 125

Gantt Chart 24, 49, 51
General Contractor 106
    & Construction Managemt 100, 101
Goal 16, 29
    long-term 28
Holdback 22, 34, 122
Information 81
    excess of 81
Inputs 16, 77 & Appendix "LFA"
Inspection 36, 80, 85, 89, 108, 115, 121, 127, 150
    factory 111
    for payments 51
Instructions 46
    in writing 164
    oral & written 97
    proper channels 46
Insurance 120
Interface 22, 57, 88, 127
    & programs 113
    & WBS 75
    authority & task 59
    of trades 50, 56, 60
LFA 19, 32, 42, 169
    & WBS 74
    evaluation of 128
Logical Framework Analysis - see LFA
Lump Sum Allowance 23, 95, 96
Mark-up 159
    cost plus 96
Milestone 25, 126
    payments 48
Network Diagrams 51, 112
Objectives 40
Organigram 25, 32, 34, 44, 67, 112, 127
    as Contract Document 45
    related to schedule & LFA 33
    & Client contract 69
    & Construction Management 103
Organization 113
Organization Chart - see Organigram
Outputs 16, 76 & Appendix LFA
Overhead 66, 67, 72
Overseas Development 83
    & WBS 76
Package 23, 79, 83, 84, 100, 109
Parameters 106
    quality, measurable 107
Payment
    terms of 92
Personnel 86, 109
    & Construction Management 102
    qualifications 110
PERT 25, 51
Plan of Operation 12, 17, 19, 20, 25, 31, 39, 75, 112, 167
    long-term 29
Plan of Operation
    budget 72
    questions & answers 32
    written 18
Planning 16, 112, 126
    long-term 28
    of documents 28

Plans & Specs. 18, 62
   clarification 52
   good & bad 52
POP - see Project Plan & Plan of Operation
Precision
   of the P.M. 15
Presentation
   of documents 27
   of information 93
Prime Cost Sum 23
Problems ignored 15
Procedures 109
   manual 120
Procurement 48
Profit 30, 41
   and overhead 49
Progress (project) 20
Project
   completion 118
   definition 25
   planning of 39
Project Management
   principles 40
Project Manager
   popularity of 117
Project plan 17, 31
Proposal 71
   as Contract Document 157
   Purchase Order 20, 90, 166
   as Contract Document 94
Purpose 16, 30, 40
Quality Assurance 105
   for Builder/GC 109
   & CM 109
   & Construction Management 108
   cost of 110
   definition 106
   fundamentals 107
   perceptions of 107
Quality Control 101, 103, 105
   & Construction Management 103
Records 21
   drawings 120
Related Work 59
Remedial work 37
Reminders 37
Renovation/Addition 12, 18, 66
   contingency 71
   contract 130
   estimating 67
   interface 88
Reputation
   establishment of 30
Request for Change 99
Resources
   human 86
Responsibility 19
   for errors 116
   for incorrect acts 45
   of the P.M. 14
Results
   & the LFA 171
Samples 151
   approvals 87
   schedule & cost 64
Schedule 32, 41, 48, 105, 110
   & WBS 75
   as Contract Document 48
   evaluation of 128
   of payments 34, 48, 50
Scope of Work 18, 33, 54, 62, 156
   contract 92
   detailed 162
   estimating 67
   how much detail? 54
   in lieu of plans & specs. 53
   interpretation 56
Shop Drawings 87, 111, 151
   control & cost 63
Site Control 85
Site Instruction 23, 36, 87, 89, 97, 98, 123, 164
   related to schedule & LFA 120
Strategic plan 17, 28, 31, 41
Sub-contract 84
Sub-contractor 23, 56, 93, 139
   & Client 94
   estimating 66
   meetings 88
   supervision 11
Substantial Completion/Performance 135
Success criteria 20
Supervision 19, 21, 127, 149
   description 90
   planning of 89
   what it includes 114
Supplementary General Conditions 152
Supplier
   accounts 72
Tender 60
   & addenda 60
Terms 21
   in proj. mgmt. 16
Things that go wrong 43
Warranty 36, 56, 118, 120, 128, 148
Work Breakdown Structure 33, 41, 51, 62, 67, 128, 172
   & Computer 81
   & cost 74
   & estimating 41
   accounts 73
   and Organigram 44
   estimating 66
Work description - see Scope of Work

BY THE SAME AUTHOR
incredibly easy project management (ISBN 0-9698126-0-4)
practical problem solving for many common management problems